MADE E-Z
PRODUCTS

Entrepreneurship

Mel Chasen

Made E-Z

MADE E-Z PRODUCTS® Inc.
Deerfield Beach, Florida / www.MadeE-Z.com

Entrepreneurship Made E-Z®
© Copyright 2002 Mel Chasen
Printed in the United States of America

Published by

MADE E-Z
PRODUCTS   384 South Military Trail
Deerfield Beach, FL 33442

http://www.MadeE-Z.com
All rights reserved.

1 2 3 4 5 6 7 8 9 10

This publication is designed to provide accurate and authoritative information in regard to subject matter covered. It is sold with the understanding that neither the publisher nor author is engaged in rendering legal, accounting, or other professional services. If legal advice or other expert assistance is required, the services of a competent professional should be sought. From: *A Declaration of Principles jointly adopted by a Committee of the American Bar Association and a Committee of Publishers.*

Entrepreneurship Made E-Z®
Mel Chasen

Limited warranty and disclaimer

This self-help product is intended to be used by the consumer for his/her own benefit. It may not be reproduced in whole or in part, resold or used for commercial purposes without written permission from the publisher.

This product is designed to provide authoritative and accurate information in regard to the subject matter covered. However, the accuracy of the information is not guaranteed, as laws and regulations may change or be subject to differing interpretations. Consequently, you may be responsible for following alternative procedures, or using material different from those supplied with this product.

Neither the author, publisher, distributor nor retailer are engaged in rendering legal, accounting or other professional services. Accordingly, the publisher, author, distributor and retailer shall have neither liability nor responsibility to any party for any loss or damage caused or alleged to be caused by the use of this product.

Copyright notice

The purchaser of this book is hereby authorized to reproduce in any form or by any means, electronic or mechanical, including photocopying, all forms and documents contained in this book, provided it is for non-profit, educational or private use. Such reproduction requires no further permission from the publisher and/or payment of any permission fee.

The reproduction of any form or document in any other publication intended for sale is prohibited without the written permission of the publisher. Publication for non-profit use should provide proper attribution to Made E-Z Products®.

To Iris:
    My best friend,
    Severest critic,
    Most ardent supporter,
    and partner in life.

Table of Contents

	Introduction 7
1.	What Is An Entrepreneur? 11
2.	Avoiding Common Mistakes 21
3.	The Spirit of Business 53
4.	The 12 Steps to Personal Success 65
5.	What Is Your Entreprenurial Potential? 91
6.	Do You Have Leadership Potential? 99
7.	Managing Your Business 115
8.	Risks, Goals, and Change 137
9.	All About Money 169
10.	Financing Your Enterprise 183
11.	The Right Style For You 197
	Appendix 209
	Resources 211
	Index 229

THE ENTREPRENEUR

*The entrepreneur is a person
who thinks change is opportunity,
and in the face of fear
moves ahead anyway,
often taking the lead.
The entrepreneur
views failure as a key
that unlocks the door of inspiration
and willingly embraces the risks
involved in taking a dream into reality.
The entrepreneur
constantly challenges the status quo
not in search of fortune or fame
but as a way to control his or her own destiny.*

Introduction

I am often asked the question, "Are entrepreneurs born or made?" This topic has been discussed and debated by educators, aspiring business people and psychologists for many years. I must admit that my own answer has varied over the years and was dependent upon where I stood at the time. If I were meeting with success, then entrepreneurs were made. If I were experiencing troubled times, then entrepreneurs were born. Now I know the correct answer: Entrepreneurs are both made and born.

Just as there are superstars in music and sports, there are outstanding entrepreneurs who have the personality and talent to build large organizations that can change the way society functions. There are also many more "regular folks," men and women who have various degrees of talent and commitment who serve in the overwhelming majority of paid positions in business and other fields. Many entrepreneurs fall into this latter category as well.

I was not born with the natural skills and personality that would make me the Beethoven of the business world. I didn't come into the world destined to be a captain of industry and the initiator of change. Only as my career developed did I begin to realize how much of the entrepreneurial spirit was hidden within my personality and character. As my career developed, so did my business skills. So did my understanding of what it takes to be a successful entrepreneur. While I was living it, my business life did not seem extraordinary or even different from that of my friends or peers. However, in retrospect, I have come to realize that it was most unusual in two respects. One was the sheer variety and number of positions I held and industries I was involved with. The other concerned the positions that I held as an executive with other companies. These positions did not give me the self-esteem or positive self image that I finally achieved when I started my own business.

During my career, I have faced a number of problems. Looking back, I can see that this was fortunate for me. Making mistakes and learning how to correct them not only sharpened my business skills, it also strengthened my resolve to learn and succeed. Becoming an entrepreneurial success isn't easy. It's not easy leaving the security of a steady paycheck or assuming full responsibility for your decisions and actions. When you're the top dog, you have no one else to blame for your failures, and there will be plenty of failures, in ways you can't imagine right now. But take solace from the fact that those failures will also provide you with the best education you can receive.

Providing you with this school-of-hard-knocks education is the reason I wrote this book in the first place. I want you to be as successful an entrepreneur as you want to be. It would give me great personal satisfaction if I could make your road a little less bumpy, curvy, and lengthy than mine was. Therefore, I have tried to present you with a clear map of the territory you are about to travel, based upon information and insights I have gleaned over my own long journey. Consider this book as a compass that points to E—Entrepreneurship.

Forget for a moment about your age, position or experience level. If you have the Entrepreneurial Fever, for which there is no cure, all those things don't matter. What does matter is that you are true to yourself. The truth of who you are and what sort of entrepreneur you will become waits to be revealed, and I hope that this book will help you uncover that truth. To that end, you will be asked some tough questions throughout the text—questions that you should answer directly and honestly. We'll be discussing such topics as morals, money, time and work ethic, and I urge you to question yourself to see where you stand on each issue.

Introduction

This book is directed toward those who might be thinking of becoming "their own boss," as well as those who have already started or taken over a business and are anxious about what the future may hold in store for them. Therefore, before you embark on the life of an entrepreneur, ask yourself if you are willing, ready and able to make a lifetime commitment to being an entrepreneur, or have already done so. The entrepreneur's life is not a nine-to-five job—it is a consuming vocation that demands constant attention and maintenance.

Perhaps once you've read this book, you'll discover that entrepreneurship isn't for you. It's too demanding, too difficult, too time-consuming, too uncertain. Well, you could find a hundred reasons for not becoming an entrepreneur. And that's okay. Many people find fulfillment working for others. But chances are that you would have never picked up a book with the word "entrepreneur" in the title if you didn't have the fever. Dave Thomas, recently deceased, was the founder of Wendy's, the famous restaurant chain. In his book, Dave's Way, he urged his readers to "find ways to be an entrepreneur;" if you are destined to be an entrepreneur, then I know you will find the means to do so.

Deciding whether or not to give in to the E-fever is your job. Mine is to help you make that decision. My closest friend, Hank Seiden, a renowned guru in the advertising field, taught me that to be effective promoting any message, you must remember three principles of communication.

1. Know whom you want to talk to.

2. Know what you want to say to your audience.

3. Know how to convey that message effectively.

I am confident that, after you have read this book, you'll find that I have satisfied my friend's doctrine, and therefore fulfilled my purpose.

What Is An Entrepreneur?

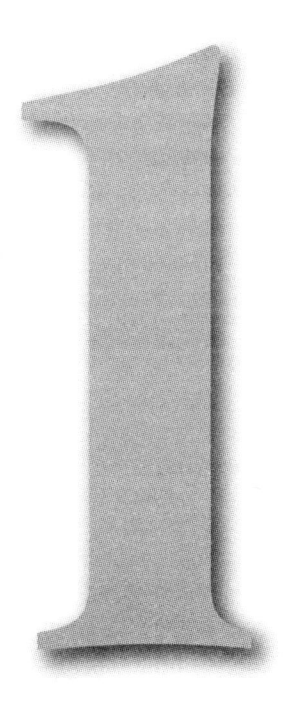

1

What Is An Entrepreneur?

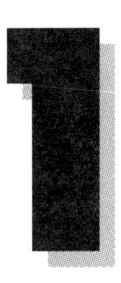

My business took over my life—by choice.
—Riva Yares

Like paint to an artist or words to a writer, business is the lifeblood of the entrepreneur. We cannot help being who and what we are anymore than artists or writers can deny who they are. Doing, developing and researching business is our chief form of creative expression. It is what we do, and those who are driven to do it cannot simply stop doing it.

But how do you know if you are truly an entrepreneur ... or just an admirer of the art? In other words, how can you tell if you have the Entrepreneurial Fever—not just the desire, but the need to be an entrepreneur? The best place to find the answer is at the beginning. So, before we examine the symptoms of the "E-fever," we had better come up with a working definition of the affliction.

Entrepreneurs have been described in many different ways. Undoubtedly, the most common and least complimentary is the notion of entrepreneurs as cold, heartless, do-anything-for-a-buck, shark-like opportunists, preying on other business people and a clueless public. Books entitled *How to Swim with the Sharks without Being Eaten* and *Nice Guys Finish Last* (the title of Leo Durocher's autobiography) do nothing to dispel this stubborn stereotype. Of course there are some ruthless business people, just as there are ruthless artists and writers, politicians, teachers, and so on. Simply put, there are ruthless people in the world, and they take up a variety of professions.

> Business has no lock on callous, uncaring behavior.

On the other hand, it is ludicrous to think that honest, trustworthy, creative people who readily share their success, listen to the needs of others, cooperate with their employees and believe in a greater purpose in life are absent from the world of business. Furthermore, their noble attributes do not hamper them in any way. On a moment's notice, I could present a laundry list of very successful business people who are good, ethical people who always give back more than they take. So, if the definition of entrepreneur isn't "a mean SOB out to make a fast buck any way he can," what exactly is it?

Over the years I've heard many attempts to define the term. Some are as complex as Joseph Schumpeter's diatribe, in which he states that entrepreneurs must be innovators who reshape patterns of production and distribution by developing new products and processes, and thereby open new markets and sources of supply. As if that weren't enough of a burden, Schumpeter also expects the entrepreneur to devise new forms of organization to handle all those innovations. This is a tall order that most entrepreneurs simply can't meet. Then there are more streamlined definitions, like that of my friend Bill, who proclaims that "Entrepreneurs are people who own their own businesses."

What Is An Entrepreneur?

It's not that I disagree with either Schumpeter or Bill, but I find that their descriptions define the extremes of what it means to be an entrepreneur. I prefer Webster's dictionary definition, which allows for different types and levels of entrepreneurs: "Entrepreneur: A person who organizes and manages an enterprise, especially a business, usually with considerable risk." Also useful is Gail Degeorge's observation that the word entrepreneur covers a "broad range of business talent." She suggests that we "place 'inventors' at one end of the spectrum, with 'implementers' on the other end and 'innovators' in the middle ...." (From her book, *The Making of a Blockbuster.*) To my way of thinking, the broad range of business talent exhibited by entrepreneurs is even wider than Degeorge suggests. More on that later.

We'll explore both the entrepreneur and the risk factors in great detail throughout the book. The following section on risk is a brief introduction to the subject.

Risk

Webster provides two definitions of risk that relate to entrepreneurs:

1. (n) exposure to the chance of loss
2. (v) to venture upon, to take a chance

Be careful, however, not to confuse the word "risky" with risk. Entrepreneurs don't go out looking for shaky, unwise business ventures, or make irresponsible decisions with the reckless aplomb of a daredevil. They take calculated risks, that is, risks that balance gains with losses. Calculated risks that result in failure generally do not result in ruin, and those that result in success can provide extravagant success. The risk may be

> Much of what entrepreneurs do is based upon taking chances—on exposing themselves to loss or even failure.

minor or major, or somewhere in between. However, people who are not entrepreneurs avoid even minor risks. The entrepreneur understands that the very act of going into business involves taking a risk. Therefore, most entrepreneurs spend a great deal of time trying to minimize risk. Either they assess the risk of any venture beforehand, or they employ "risk managers" to minimize risk and prevent catastrophic loss.

Knowing that you will take a risk simply by going into business for yourself, you must ask yourself how great a risk you are willing to take, while recognizing that there are varying levels of risk. Every entrepreneur I know is different in terms of the degree of risk he or she will tolerate. Being high or low on the tolerance scales is neutral, neither good nor bad. A high tolerance doesn't mean that a person is going to be any better at owning and operating a business than someone with a low tolerance. Risk tolerance simply indicates the type of business you should choose and how big or quickly that business will grow.

> Understanding and honestly evaluating your risk tolerance is the essential first step in determining what kind of entrepreneur you are.

The question of risk is very different for the entrepreneur contemplating it as opposed to those who may be evaluating it (such as investors, friends, and banks). An entrepreneur may have his or her entire fortune balanced on taking a risk, while the others usually do not. Therefore it is important to take the following factors into consideration to determine your risk tolerance:

- Your past experience and knowledge.
- The risk/reward ratio, relative to time and capital. In other words, what do you stand to gain over and above your investment in time and money? What do you stand to lose?

What Is An Entrepreneur?

- The results of a thorough investigation of the service or product you wish to supply and the competition that may already exist.
- The production of a realistic business plan.
- The ability to secure or provide adequate capital.
- Your level of confidence in your ability to lead and be resourceful in the face of unforeseen setbacks.

After you have considered all the above factors, read the following stories about people (myself included) representing high, medium and low risks, and the results of the various ventures. Hopefully these case histories will help you determine where you stand regarding risk tolerance. (Note that this section does not include dot.com failures, which I consider to be a special case. We'll discuss that topic in a separate section.)

High Risk

In this category about the farthest extremes of risk, it would be easy to pinpoint many failures. However, I have chosen to highlight the following, less common successes.

Fred Smith and Federal Express

When he was a junior in college, Mr. Smith wrote a term paper in which he basically envisioned what would ultimately become Federal Express. Based upon his observation of the need for fast delivery service, his knowledge and love of flying, as well as his unshakable confidence in the concept itself, he invested his own net worth (about eight million dollars) in the project. He also persuaded banks and investors to supply more than 80 million, bringing the total of the investment to 90 million dollars. At the time, 1971, this was the largest single venture-capital start-up in history. We all know how well it paid off. By the way, the professor who graded Mr. Smith's paper was unimpressed by his arguments and gave the paper a "C."

Mel Chasen and Transmedia Network Inc.

Since this is my own story, I can assure you of its complete accuracy. I started this project at age 56, after a varied and extensive period of "on-the-job training." Without that kind of background, I can honestly admit that this venture would probably not have been successful.

In 1984, several investors and I established a company called Transmedia Network Inc. that supplied its members with a convenient and dignified way to save money at high-end restaurants without using embarrassing discount coupons. Instead, Transmedia members paid for their meals with a private label charge card. In order to enlist restaurants in the program, we supplied them with funds in return for meal credits, which are called "rights to receive."

Transmedia's success was based upon a three-pronged approach. We had balanced a benefit (cardholders saving money and dignity) against a need (the restaurants' need for cash and customers) and executed a program that addressed both.

> Over 11 years, Transmedia grew from an idea backed by minimal funding to an NYSE company with more than 100 million dollars in volume.

Medium risk

I personally know a man who spent his career starting and building a very successful and profitable vending business. Although he had no business training, he had a strong work ethic and the business instinct to build slowly and to buy smaller routes and new equipment as they became available. In this slow but steady manner, he developed a strong cash flow and a profitable company. I consider his venture a "medium risk," as opposed to a low

What Is An Entrepreneur?

risk, because he did not stagnate or rest on his laurels. He kept adding assets in order to expand his existing business.

This man sold his business to a public company. Well after the "waiting time" mandated in his contract, he started a similar business with his son. Because of changes within the vending industry, they shifted their focus to include retail operations, pay telephones, and related ventures. The founder passed away, but his son continues the same pattern of constant, conservative expansion and flexibility that his father taught him, and it has paid off handsomely.

Low risk
(as viewed by the entrepreneur)

A young woman that I know, who is an accountant and a lawyer, has worked for both a large and medium accounting firm, as well as a middle-sized law firm. She recently decided to control her own destiny by opening her own practice. She did this by providing counsel to an existing firm and bartering some of her legal and accounting services to pay for her rent and utilities. Thanks to her past experience involving a broad range of clients, she is doing quite well, and has made almost no capital investments. Most of all, she is pleased to be in control of her own fate.

> Assessing the level of risk in a decision to enter, buy or start a business is not always an obvious proposition.

So much depends upon the qualifications of the individual entrepreneur—his or her training, personality, leadership qualities, experience, and his or her awareness of his or her own capabilities and character. All this forms the basis of a business.

Only by evaluating all the criteria can you truly understand and honestly contemplate the amount of risk involved in any given enterprise and whether or not you can tolerate that amount of risk. Bear in mind that as your experience and knowledge grow, propositions that you once considered to be "high risk" will become "medium" or "low risk." Surprisingly, the opposite is also true.

Avoiding Common Mistakes

2

Avoiding Common Mistakes

The greatest danger for the new venture is to "know better" than the customer what the product or service is or should be, how it should be bought, and what it should be used for.
—Peter Drucker

Before you discover what to do to become a successful entrepreneur, it's probably a good idea to learn what not to do. This in itself is a giant step toward understanding how entrepreneurship works—and doesn't work. The following is a list of 10 all-too-common errors made by inexperienced entrepreneurs and even, occasionally, experienced businessmen and women who should know better. Any one of these mistakes could seriously endanger—if not prevent—your entrepreneurial success. A combination of them is almost always lethal, even to the most original concept and well-conceived marketing plan.

The Ten Most Common Errors of Entrepreneurs

1. Failure to provide a needed product or service

2. Lack of knowledge about the chosen industry

3. Failure to establish a realistic business plan

4. Inability to manage people

5. Lack of leadership or character necessary to inspire confidence

6. Focus on one grand success instead of gradually building success in increments

7. Establishment of commitments without a plan to fulfill them

8. Focus on personal needs (perks, cash, etc.) before business needs

9. Failure to focus on sales and collections

10. Failure to provide for advertising and promotion

Avoiding Common Mistakes

Let's examine each error separately, beginning with what may very well be the most serious.

Error number one

Failure to provide a needed product or service

This error highlights the heart of what it means to be an entrepreneur. Whether you are starting a business from scratch, or interested in buying an existing business, learn to recognize the many forms of this error so you can avoid making it.

> Generally speaking, the more people or companies who share the need—and thus require it to be fulfilled with your product or service—the better.

Let's look at a famous entrepreneur who did succeed by paying attention to his customers' needs and demands. Long before he began manufacturing ketchup, R. J. Heinz gained fame as a supplier of horseradish. He took pride in producing a fresh, wholesome product based upon his mother's recipe, but because horseradish was sold in amber-colored jars in the 19th century, it was impossible to distinguish Heinz's fresh product from that of less reputable competitors. Shoppers would open a new, opaque bottle of a rival's horseradish, only to discover that it was discolored and spoiled.

Heinz lost no time in responding to the needs of the consumer and highlighting the quality of his product at the same time. He began to market his products in clear glass bottles, allowing housewives to see at a glance that Heinz had nothing to hide. His products were always fresh and appetizing, unlike those of his competition. Heinz showed that he cared more about meeting his customers' concerns than about making a fast buck or unloading questionable goods. He used his intuition to understand his customers' needs to know about the product before they purchased it. He then used logic to meet that need and develop the public's trust.

To paraphrase a quotation from Peter Drucker, businesses are not paid to reform customers. They are paid to satisfy customers. Of course, it's not always easy to spot a consumer demand or to interpret it correctly. Sometimes entrepreneurs jump on a bandwagon without looking to see whether or not it has wheels. For example, in recent years, creating scrapbooks became a popular pastime for many, especially invalids and senior citizens. This trend inspired whole product lines of stickers, papers, rubber stamps, and pens before marketers actually sat down, thought about the audience and the very nature of a scrapbook, and asked themselves, "Are we really fulfilling the market's needs with these products?"

The answer was, in a word, no. Many of the people keeping this kind of album were ill or older people on a fixed income—people who could not afford fancy, unnecessary stationery items. Some were not even able to go out shopping for them. In addition, a scrapbook is primarily a collection of non-manufactured "scraps"—notes, letters, photographs, newspaper articles, written anecdotes, drawings, ribbons, pressed flowers and the like—all available at little or no cost. These items have personal meaning and sentimental value to one or two individuals or at most a family. Pricey, mass-produced, impersonal, glossy decorations are, in a fundamental sense, counterproductive to the creation of such a personal, private, individual collection. As a result, such products were a very hard sell to those who neither needed nor wanted them.

Remember when fruit juicers were all the rage—for about three months in the early 1990s? These expensive gadgets turned half a dozen oranges into fresh juice in a few seconds, a fascinating capability. But did a lot of people

Avoiding Common Mistakes

> Trouble also arises when an entrepreneur confuses providing a feature with providing a benefit.

really want or need it? Juicers were touted as a "revolution" in healthy eating, allowing people to make small or large amounts of fresh fruit and vegetable juice quickly and easily. This claim was true, up to a point, until people using these machines realized that while fresh fruit is almost as expensive as fresh juice, and perfectly healthy, delicious juice is readily available at very reasonable prices. In addition to their initial expense, juicers also require a significant time investment when it comes to cleanup, especially when one has to clean a large, complicated machine after juicing a single pear.

Juicers provided a benefit, but that benefit was fairly small compared to the expense and effort that the product required. Juicers are still available, but they are certainly not necessities for most people, largely because their limited benefits are canceled out by negatives. The same holds true for

> Try to avoid the siren song of products and services when they appear clever and sexy, but don't fill a real need, offer a compelling benefit or are simply more trouble than they are worth.

yogurt makers, food processors, and other machines that offer convenience and time-savings with one hand and take them away with the other.

Error number two

Lack of knowledge about the chosen industry

If you are creating or promoting a product or service for a specific industry, acquire a thorough understanding of that industry before you try to sell it a specific concept. This is certainly true if you are taking over an existing company, but even more crucial if you are trying to break into an industry with a new company. By "thorough understanding" I don't mean just the industry's products or services, advertising and profit goals. I mean the intricacies of just how that industry works on a daily basis, and what your role and responsibilities will be.

Bernie was a successful computer engineer who had a gift for designing cutting-edge software. Deciding that he didn't want to work for anyone any more, he looked for an existing business to own and operate. After an extensive search, Bernie chose to use his life savings and inheritance to buy a landscape company with 100 employees. The business served an affluent area of South Florida and had many established customers, so Bernie was certain that it would do well.

But Bernie had never managed more than 10 people at a time, had never worked in a landscaping business, and, in fact, knew absolutely nothing about plants and lawns, except that they needed to be watered and trimmed now and then. He really didn't understand the needs of the staff, the demanding scheduling challenges, or the challenges of maintaining a fleet of trucks, mowers, and support equipment. Bernie and his wife had only lived in the U.S. about five or six years and, although they were both well-educated, they were not completely fluent in English, a fact that hampered their negotiations with their very wealthy customers. Since the business was located about an hour away from their home, they decided to move in order to be closer to the business. On

> You must know the intricacies of any business that you are undertaking before you undertake it, whether you are starting a business from scratch or taking over the reins of an existing business.

Avoiding Common Mistakes

top of all these challenges, Bernie had never worked in sales. He never had to bring in business before. Worst of all, Bernie did not understand that, in the lawn care industry, clients often paid in cash that didn't always find its way to the bottom line. He discovered, belatedly, that the books had been doctored to make the business appear far better in terms of cash flow than it actually was. You can probably guess what happened. In less than three years, the $150,000 that Bernie had invested had disappeared and the business folded.

Bernie's disastrous adventure illustrates an important point. Even if you are familiar with some aspects of the enterprise you are starting or taking over, you may still not be knowledgeable enough to actually make the business a success. There are many questions you will have to answer, including: What are your start-up costs? Your day-to-day costs? Who are your customers? Your competitors?

Learning a business through on-the-job training is a rare gift, however, and I wouldn't count on having it. Most of us poor mortals will have to do a lot of research to master the information that is critical to giving us a solid understanding—and appreciation—of an industry and how it functions. Your needs and desires don't count here, except for your desire to succeed. What matters are the needs of the customers whom you and the industry are trying to reach.

> Now, there are a very few, highly talented entrepreneurs who can learn a business through on-the-job training.

Sometimes you can use the experiences you acquired from working in one business to help you overcome your lack of familiarity in a new business. A willingness to ask questions of seasoned players in your new industry—and listen to their answers—can also help you avoid disaster.

That's what I did when I was given the responsibility of running the casino at Caesar's Palace in Las Vegas. As president of the company that owned the hotel, circumstances beyond my control had placed me in an unusual position. Although I had been a customer at the casinos, and not a very successful customer either, I must admit, I had never managed a casino before. The casino was not producing the profit level that we expected from each type of game. I was charged with the twin duties of discovering why the problem existed *and* turning it around.

On my first walk through the floor of the casino, a few people familiar with its operations went with me. They pointed out some of the tricks used by customers to beat the house—with and without the help of the employees. The world of the casino was different from any other business I had ever experienced. Most of the employees never saw the light of day. There were no windows, no doors, no clock, and I quickly lost my sense of time.

I soon realized that I could never learn to monitor the casino with my limited background alone. I simply did not know the industry. I had no idea how much profit the various games—dice, blackjack, roulette and baccarat—were supposed to generate. I also did not know the *hold* of each game. That is, how much money was supposed to be left at the end of the day, after paying the winners. (It turns out that holds vary slightly from game to game.) There was nothing in my background that would help me understand these crucial details.

I tried to hire one of the industry's leaders to run our casino, but he declined, as he was working elsewhere at the time. Fortunately, he did tell me what to expect in terms of the average hold from each game. Seeking help from other experts in the field, I met with my own executives, men named Wingy, Mokey and Ash—names that did little to inspire my confidence in the industry. Their information

Avoiding Common Mistakes

dovetailed with what I had recently learned, and together we calculated the percentages that each game should have been producing. I put Wingy, Mokey and Ash in charge of the games on the floor in order to ensure that these games generated the calculated holdings. Based upon my experience with salespeople in the vending industry who had their own routes, I put each supervisor in his own "business" and told him he was now responsible for achieving the desired results. Sure enough, with my team of experts on the job, we began to meet our numbers.

> We each bring something to the table from our past experience—something we can apply to a new situation, business or industry.

Use what you know, and at the same time, get as much expert advice as possible so that you can successfully adapt the skills and experiences you have already acquired to the demands of the new business environment you have just entered.

Error number three

Failure to establish a realistic business plan

This error is most commonly made by those entrepreneurs just starting up a new business. The problem arises when business people fail to focus on the day-to-day growth and establishment of the enterprise. Worse yet, they may be unable to explain or express their business strategies and goals clearly and effectively.

In order to avoid these errors, you, as an entrepreneur beginning a new venture or taking over an existing one, must first picture yourself in the future, engaged in company business. Then you must ask yourself the following questions: What will you do on each day? How much business will you bring in? What sort of rent would you be willing to pay? Where and how would you sell your product and to whom would you sell it? You as an entrepreneur must have a clear idea of what your business will be before you actually go about doing business. That is the key behind the creation of a solid business plan.

After you have addressed these fundamental functions, it is necessary to record them in writing as clearly and simply as possible. You may know each step of your business plan, but that is not good enough. You will need a clear, comprehensive document that you and others can refer to.

Now, it is time to assess your capital and assign costs to each of the fundamental functions. In addition, you will have to assign a potential income from some of the functions, always calculating an amount for reserve. These might seem like obvious necessities. The trouble is that it is not always easy to determine how much money is sufficient for any given stage of business development. Also, at any step of the way, you may encounter costs that you had not foreseen.

> Don't try to start or grow a business without the funds necessary to do so.

I will be going into details about business plans in a later section, but I want to provide you with a vivid example of what can happen if you do not create a realistic business plan and fail to provide for sufficient funds.

In the mid-1990s, dot.com companies ruled the stock market. Fortunes were made or destroyed at the click of a mouse, or so it seemed. Most of these companies, however, had little or nothing to sell. They did not fill any need or provide a service, and usually did not have a clear-cut method of achieving a positive cash flow. The public wasn't really interested in their economics (and neither were the analysts, in many cases). Their solvency depended upon the

Avoiding Common Mistakes

next round of financing and the prices of their stock. Those who voiced any skepticism were called "old financial" and told that they did not understand the new economy. Of course, the counter-criticism stopped suddenly when the dot.coms tanked after a few years of wild, unearned success.

> It is necessary to write a business plan—a roadmap—to determine where you are going wrong, where you are going right, and how you can correct your deficiencies.

If I may get personal for a moment, I do believe that the beginning of Transmedia Network embodied the opposite of the dot.coms' slipshod planning. My associates and I had a strong business plan for how we were going to achieve results, even though we did not have an existing model. While we made some mistakes, we also had some strong back-up financing ideas that saw us through some of the toughest times.

Error number four

Inability to manage people effectively

This section deals mainly with errors in working with people. In the vast majority of cases, you will not be able to survive alone as an entrepreneur, except, perhaps, at the very start of the company. As the company grows, you'll need people to handle product, to staff the office, and to manage and organize services. If you try to run the business alone, chances are that you'll find yourself beset by tasks and assignments that eat up your time and undermine your sense of focus. It is better to delegate these tasks to an employee.

Are you an artist, writer or musician? If so, you, to an important extent, are the product. Your paintings, books and music are extensions of yourself. Perhaps you'll need an assistant, apprentice or publicist, or perhaps you can manage alone. If your skills are the focus of your business, then it becomes more difficult to delegate authority for aspects of

> Whether you have one employee or a hundred or more depends a great deal upon the product or service you are promoting.

that business. A talented writer, for example, may pay someone to do research, as the famous novelist James Michener did, but it's not likely that he will pay a ghostwriter to do his writing for him.

Let's say that, like most entrepreneurs, you require a certain number of employees to do certain, specialized tasks that you have neither the training nor time to handle. The moment of truth, I believe, comes at the point of hiring, not later down the line. Can you trust the people you hire to assist you? Is their background more than adequate for the job? Are they either experienced or clearly capable of on-the-job training? If they are, then you have a job, too—you must trust them to handle their own work.

Too often an entrepreneur fails as a manager of his own employees because he cannot really let go of the work he has performed for so long himself. He cannot delegate authority effectively, and this stems from the fact that he doesn't really trust his employees to do as good a job as he would. "After all, it's merely a job to them," our hypothetical entrepreneur might say. "They didn't start the business from the ground up the way I did. They can't have my level of commitment."

It is important to realize that *no one* is going to be as committed to your venture as you will be. It's not your employees' baby—it's yours. Your employees know this, even if you don't, and are looking to you for initial guidance, acceptance, encouragement, and most, of all, the freedom to perform their jobs without hindrance.

I recall a man named Richard, an excellent salesman in the media buying business, who had created a profitable company. However, he paid absolutely no attention to the details of his company, and it required a great deal of attention, especially when it came to fiscal responsibilities, such as collecting outstanding receivables. While Richard continued to sell, he built a bloated organization that ultimately collapsed, and he had to declare bankruptcy. Unfortunately, as brilliant as he might have been in sales, he did not realize that even though you delegate authority in a specific area to another person, you never relinquish your ultimate responsibility as the owner.

When a problem arises, a manager is on top of the situation immediately in order to correct it, or, in the best of all worlds, prevents the problem from arising in the first place. To do this, he must know his or her employees, be familiar with their work on a day-to-day basis, and willing to take responsibility for any deviation from the norm. Because Richard did not realize that he had the ultimate responsibility for the health of his company, he suffered the ultimate business heartache. While his employees lost their jobs, he lost his company. I have always followed this principle: hire slowly, fire quickly (if you have made an error in judgement) and be generous in severance.

Error number five

Lack of leadership or character necessary to inspire confidence

Richard failed as a leader of his employees, and an entrepreneur is above all else a leader. He or she is the champion for the product or service he or she is trying to promote. He or she is its knight on a white horse, and without his or her efforts, the product will probably go nowhere. His or her associates may help him or her, but

Entrepreneurship Made E-Z

ultimately the buck stops with him or her. As Richard found out the hard way, a huge amount of responsibility rests on a leader's shoulders. If he or she is not a person of foresight, scruples, honor, integrity, courage and determination, his or her associates and clients will lose faith in him or her, and, by extension, the product he or she represents.

While it is the mark of an entrepreneur to be determined and competitive and to have the courage of his or her convictions, this does not mean that "anything goes" in order to achieve the desired ends. I believe that an entrepreneur can and should work within the framework of traditional ethics in order to succeed. Doing so, he or she brings success not only to himself or herself, but to those around him or her.

> Conventional wisdom often portrays the entrepreneur as an egomaniac, not just devoted to his or her ideas but obsessed by the notion of being right—of having his or her own way, at any cost.

Sometimes the failure to lead effectively creates shocking lapses in ethics and respect for basic human rights when business places profit before people. One such example plagued a major food company throughout the 1960s, '70s, and '80s. In order to maximize sales of infant formula in developing countries, company agents encouraged local mothers to cease breast feeding their infants and switch to the commercial formula, which needed to be mixed with water. Since the formula was expensive, and local sources of water were often contaminated, infant mortality in these nations soared. A worldwide boycott of this company's products finally stopped this practice, but not before many infants succumbed to needless malnutrition and water poisoning.

On the other hand, here is an example of how a major company handled a crisis with sensitivity, courage, and

Avoiding Common Mistakes

urgency. In the early 1980s, three people died from cyanide introduced into capsules of the pain reliever, Extra Strength Tylenol. The link between the deaths and the capsules was made very quickly, presenting Johnson & Johnson, the manufacturers of Tylenol, with a dilemma. Tylenol, a major brand, accounted for a great part of the corporation's income. Despite warnings from the stock analysts and investors concerning the probability of tremendous political and financial loss, the company acted quickly to pull the product off the retail shelves. Johnson & Johnson's credo begins with the following statement, "We believe that our first responsibility is to the doctors, nurses, patients, and to the mothers and all others who use our product or services." Although some financial loss did occur as predicted, the company won back most of its market share in a relatively short period, and was instrumental in the development of tamper-proof containers. Unfortunately, the public too often hears about the lack of morals in the business world, and not about the many moral and ethical executives and entrepreneurs.

Error number six

Focus on one grand success instead of gradually building success in increments

A word to the wise here: Disney World was not built in a day. It takes time to grow a success, and, despite a few spectacular exceptions, the larger the success, the more time and planning it takes to create it.

> The road to success is full of small, mundane details and activities, and the wise entrepreneur would do well to pay attention to them.

Our society extols all that is instant, or at least quick: fast food, rapid transit, instant gratification, instant latte. But the

Entrepreneurship Made E-Z

truth is, in business, big successes usually come one small step at a time. At some point in the process, a product or service will "catch fire" and attract the attention of a large market, but this is usually after it has been around for a while, making its presence known and building a solid word-of-mouth reputation. You might say that it takes years to become an "overnight success."

To think that you can "instantly" fill a need or sell a market on a product or service is very naïve. It does happen, of course, but instant success is the exception, not the rule. Earlier, we discussed dot.com companies and their "instant"—but basically groundless and temporary—success. Today, those companies who survived the crash of the dot.coms are now rebuilding, trying to achieve success one pragmatic step at a time instead of trying to do too much, too quickly.

While it is important to have a far-reaching vision of the company and its path to success, too much concentration upon the big picture and not enough attention to daily details sets the stage for failure. Imagine being the captain of the Titanic, ignoring icebergs lurking beneath the surface of the ocean while basking in the glory of commanding an "indestructible" ship that you believe will change the entire future of shipbuilding. You want to avoid that trap.

> It is a mistake to look "too far ahead" in any aspect of one's business and thus neglect the day-to-day needs and activities that are often at the heart of any corporation.

A former associate of mine likes to tell a story to illustrate the importance of a step-by-step, practical transition from next-to-nothing to modest success. After WWII, he was in the business of buying surplus properties, and once had the occasion to purchase 300 cases of searchlight bulbs. He wasn't sure how he was going to market them, but he had

Avoiding Common Mistakes

the instincts to realize that he could make a profit from them at some future date. He showed his bulbs to two interested salespeople, one who had connections with Woolworth & Co., and another—a "little guy"—who sold bulbs to small retail outlets and local stores from the back of his truck. The Woolworth rep assured my friend that he would be able to take the entire load of bulbs within the next month and make a handsome profit for all concerned. The little guy could not take the entire caseload, but offered to "take a couple of cases and see what I can do." Over the next four months, the Woolworth's rep had not sold a single bulb, while the little guy sold the entire lot, four or five cases at a time. My friend said he learned a lesson from the experience. Sometimes it pays not to go after the grand success, but to achieve success one small step at a time.

Those small, important, pesky details—Not everyone is a "detail person," that is, someone who not only sees the big picture, but also sees and enjoys the many details that go into forming that big picture. This skill is something like composing an illustration of a large, central image out of a collage of hundreds of small photographs. Riding herd on important business details and keeping all these critical little "ducks in a row" is one of the main activities of an entrepreneur's day-to-day work life. If you ever need to prove your honesty or recover funds or protect your back, you'll be glad you kept accurate records of your details.

> If you do not enjoy detail work, I suggest that you try to overcome your aversion to it.

Every business, particularly in its early stages, is encumbered by details that, though seemingly minor, are necessary to future success. Some examples of small, daily, mundane details that must be taken care of on an ongoing basis are as follows: planning, location, supply and procurement, manufacturing, advertising, legalities and procedures, marketing, shipping, and distribution. These are all are driven by their own individual agendas, as well as the larger vision of the company.

One of the most important mundane activities involves keeping track of income for expected cash, the amounts expended, and the amounts received. It is also important to record the following details about these transactions:

- The dates upon which all transactions are received
- The comparison prices for such services as printing, rent, telephone use, and so on
- Contracts with customers or clients who are involved in these transactions
- Details of the contracts, including the clients' abilities to meet the terms of the contracts and their adherence to the contracts

Having employees creates another area of crucial day-to-day work. You'll need to supervise your employees and work with them, taking care not to hinder or inhibit their abilities. On the contrary, you want to encourage them to use their abilities as fully and effectively as possible. At the same time, you will need to evaluate your employees and help them attain their highest level of job performance.

Error number seven

Establishment of commitments without a plan to execute them

Taking on too many projects or duties, or focusing too hard on grandiose ideas, can lead an entrepreneur to act like a bad politician and make promises he knows he can't keep. Before long, he'll find himself swamped with impossible deadlines and unrealistic goals, as well as dozens of people

Avoiding Common Mistakes

threatening to turn him into mincemeat if he doesn't come through on his pledge. You'd be surprised at how quickly one promising project can generate too much potential business, which too often translates into lost opportunities.

> Think big and plan big, if you wish, but before you act, be sure that you can execute those magnificent ideas and extensive plans.

John was an importer and marketer of stuffed toys who appeared to be at the right place at the right time with the right product. His business was doing well, but not spectacularly, when a young koala bear at a large, urban zoo became ill. The zoo solicited funds for the animal's treatment, and children from all over the country responded, raising over a $100,000 for little Kolly. John, realizing the opportunity, pressed his foreign sources to concentrate on producing toy koala bears exclusively. Securing permission from the zoo to use Kolly's name, John began the massive job of distributing the plush dolls in a large chain of discount department stores. The toys soon sold out, and John looked to be well on his way to a major success.

Unfortunately, John was blinded by his initial success and did not know when to pull back and regroup. Boldly charging ahead, he began to solicit for other opportunities involving Kolly products, and soon was inundated with demands for books, school supplies, keychains, animated cartoons, and other products he was not familiar with. If John had had more time, better contacts, or a comprehensive business plan, he might have been able to meet these varied commitments. Because he had failed to plan for a best-case scenario, deadlines passed him by and projects fell through the cracks. By the time he had the necessary manufacturers and distributors in place, the craze for Kolly products had come to an abrupt end, replaced by the "next big thing." John's entire window of opportunity was about four months, with the peak of demand lasting only three weeks. Even his initial import business had hit the skids, since his product sources were still consumed with turning out obsolete product.

You can learn from John's mistakes. Be aware that when opportunity knocks, you are either prepared to handle every contingency or accept only a share of the spoils. Otherwise, you may be unable to meet unrealistic demands and, thus, suffer a devastating loss.

Don't confuse concept and execution. These two are not the same, and you need both in order to succeed in business. No matter how great or original a concept is, it simply won't work if your execution is shoddy, inappropriate or incomplete. John had a good concept, but his execution was haphazard and disorganized. That, along with his over-commitments, destroyed his hopes for success.

Sometimes, when a business expands too rapidly, an entrepreneur can find himself wearing too many hats, making too many promises, and riding out in too many different directions. Sales is a particularly vulnerable area. The following story illustrates how one company was able to handle mounting responsibilities in a wise manner.

> The entrepreneur can delegate duties, but if he has more responsibility than he can handle, certain areas of the business can go unattended.

The Challenge Pet Care Company specialized in making special beds and other equipment for old or ailing dogs and cats. The company was growing and beginning to show a profit when the Board of Directors was urged to hire a "lieutenant," or right-hand man, to assume some of the duties of the overburdened founder. Unfortunately, the

Avoiding Common Mistakes

company could not afford to hire a person of the caliber required for such a job. Realizing that he needed to meet the company's most crucial commitments first, the founder analyzed his business and discovered that sales was the area that was most important to the company's growth. He promptly hired a sales manager, a move that allowed the founder to concentrate on other commitments while still attending to the crucial area of sales. The founder hoped to groom the sales manager for the "lieutenant" position, but even if his plans fell through, at least he had taken precautions to help the company keep growing.

As your company grows and takes on more commitments, you must be sure you can process all of them properly. Hire people you can trust, and then trust them to do their jobs. Don't forget the conventional wisdom: You can't be all things to all people. Recognize your strengths, then focus on those particular areas.

Error number eight

Focus on personal needs instead of business needs

This mistake is all too common among first-time entrepreneurs as well as "intrapreneurs" such as company executives or other employees with a great deal of responsibility. Too often business owners develop an "employee mindset" that focuses on benefits, perks, incentives and other goodies specifically aimed at rewarding an individual who meets or exceeds a predetermined goal. But you are the business owner. Your incentive should be your dream of creating a viable, growing business, *not* receiving a bonus in your pay envelope.

> Many people take on the role of an entrepreneur, or would like to, because they connect the term with wealth and power. And they are right, up to a point.

Entrepreneurship Made E-Z

People of influence who have not inherited fame, riches or power probably used their business skills to create a successful company, or even a business "empire" like Wendy's or Microsoft. But success didn't happen overnight. It took the great entrepreneurs a lot of effort, many sleepless nights, significant initial investment and often years of worry, rejection, and self-doubt to grow their massive businesses from small, often risky ventures.

The truth is that being an entrepreneur is often a lonely, weary and underpaid profession, at least in the early years, and sometimes that start-up period extends well beyond the owner's early forecasts. Unforeseen events—union troubles, slowdowns in the economy, changes in social trends, even bad weather—can cause business setbacks and delays. Typically, successful entrepreneurs pay their employees first and themselves last, and often they don't pay themselves more than the bare minimum needed to survive. Instead, they recycle any available funds back into the business to help sustain it or grow it.

> In general, a focus on personal needs and the appearance of wealth contradicts the "unspoken motto" of the true entrepreneur—business success first, personal success second.

The all-consuming "need" of most entrepreneurs is to use their spirit of independence to build a successful business enterprise, or even a string of separate enterprises. Traditional "perks" such as spacious offices, plush furnishings, a corporate car or plane, or financial bonuses usually mean nothing to them until the business has become well established. Only then do they feel financially secure enough to sample the fruits of their efforts. On the other hand, some entrepreneurs are never comfortable in flaunting their success and maintain a lifestyle that appears modest on the surface. They know that pursuing and

Avoiding Common Mistakes

emphasizing the accumulation of luxuries will only distract them from their goal of establishing a vibrant, highly profitable business.

I'd like to tell you two stories to illustrate these two extremes. I know a man nicknamed "Hotshot" who worked for a vending company and eventually bought the business for himself. He decided that now he was a substantial entrepreneur, and therefore needed all the trappings of success. These included expensive automobiles, designer clothing, and, of course, a high salary. As the business encountered trouble, he began to borrow money to support his company, and, of course, his lavish lifestyle. When his accountant warned him that money was getting tight and suggested that he give up his perks, Hotshot felt so offended that he rushed out to buy another Italian suit to add to his magnificent wardrobe. The net result of his wasteful extravagance was that he ran his company straight into bankruptcy.

On the other hand, I have a long-standing friendship with a man who has become extremely wealthy. Once, when on a business trip, a car rental agency refused to honor his corporate discount. He then traveled half an hour away to another agency, which accepted the discount. But because he was as honorable as he was thrifty, when he took my family and me to dinner the next day, he paid the cost himself instead of charging it to his business account. This gracious man had the ability and understanding to make sure that he spent his riches wisely and honestly, putting his company first and his lifestyle second. I suggest that you try to follow his example.

Error number nine

Failure to pay attention to sales and collections

No matter how scrupulously you avoid all the other nine common errors, if you don't focus upon making sales and collecting the subsequent payments, your enterprise will fail. Of that I have not one iota of doubt. Why? Because sales and collections supply the means for you to grow or even just maintain your company. Without them, it is virtually impossible to continue to invest in your business and expand it.

> Too often, financial disaster is caused when entrepreneurs ignore sales and collections.

Paying attention to sales sounds fundamental, but I've seen many otherwise intelligent people ignore this aspect of their business. I know of one man who got so involved in cost controls and systems that he forgot the importance of securing new accounts and maintaining his existing ones. His sales dropped, but at least his systems showed him exactly what was wrong, and how he was going out of business by losing business. He ultimately had to sell out.

Here's another shocker: A sale is not the end of a negotiation. After making a big sale, a businessperson has a tendency to relax and celebrate. So much tension has been built up prior to getting that customer's final signature on the dotted line of the order form that any release of tension feels like a triumph. In truth, however, making a sale, even a big sale, is equivalent to catching your breath before tackling a difficult task. A sale is a promise to pay, and the sale is not complete until you have been paid. Just like a marriage that has not been consummated, a sale is a pledge to do something. It shouldn't be confused with the "something" itself.

Avoiding Common Mistakes

You could theoretically set a new record for sales and still go belly-up. That's because, in order to eventually show a profit, you will have to collect on those sales. Too often, hard-charging entrepreneurs forget the importance of this crucial step and fail to follow up on sales.

I once knew a co-owner of a public relations agency that had a very large account. The account's payments were in arrears but it continued to use the agency. Sure enough, over time this client built up a very large receivable. The agency carried the receivable, thereby putting itself in grave jeopardy. Finally my friend went to the client, demanding payment in no uncertain terms. The agency did collect its money, but it eventually lost the account. This was no great loss, as it turned out. The freeloading client hired a different agency which was soon stuck with a huge receivable that was not collectable.

> By overextending credit, you put yourself and your customer in fiscal jeopardy.

Just because a client has a prestigious name or reputation is no reason to neglect collecting for his or her sales. If a customer cannot pay immediately, set up a reasonable payment schedule, then be sure to follow through on it.

Error Number Ten

Failure to provide for advertising and promotion

I once had a friend who had been an advertising copywriter for many years. During one of our many discussions about the topic of business advertising, I asked him if he thought that business owners valued good advertising very highly. First he gave me a big laugh, then he said, "Unfortunately not. In fact, in every ad agency I've ever worked for, we used to joke that the minute an account's profits seemed to be going south, advertising was the first item to be reduced. Sometimes it was even dropped from the budget entirely. A whole lot of otherwise smart business people don't really understand how important advertising is to the success of their company, and it's a damn shame."

I could sympathize with my friend's position. I've seen a lot of businesses get into huge trouble by not advertising when they needed to, or by advertising in very ineffective ways, or by spending far too much money and energy on advertising when it wasn't necessary. This includes money used for effective advertising. Keep in mind that a budget for excellent advertising and promotion is money well-spent.

> Sometimes the old adage prevails: You must spend money in order to make money.

To start with, let's examine the difference between advertising and promotion. While they are often equated, advertising is commonly associated with the use of private advertising agencies hired to write and create print ads, brochures, TV commercials, and the like. You can use the creative work of advertising agencies to announce a new product or service, reposition an old one, or update customers on product improvements. Besides print and broadcast ads, direct mail campaigns, event planning and trade shows, and even speech-writing can all be effective forms of advertising.

Not all companies need advertising, but virtually all require some kind of promotion, that is, getting the word out about the company to prospective customers. Promotion is also a general term used to describe all advertising, but it is often thought of as self-promotion, in which a company promotes itself without the use of an outside agent. Self-promotion techniques include product giveaways, telemarketing and cold calling, in-store events,

Avoiding Common Mistakes

classified ads and other forms of local advertising, to name a few. For example, a new candy company could send free samples of its product to homeowners in a certain city or larger area, or a new bagel shop could stage a grand opening with free coffee, buy-one-get-one-free (BOGO) coupons, and other value-added inducements to buy. Other new stores will stage grand openings featuring other inducements, such as sales, entertainment and premiums.

> Self-promotion is often less expensive than other forms of advertising, but it frequently demands significant effort and planning from the entrepreneur.

For a sample of effective advertising, consider an early Mercedes-Benz campaign. This luxury auto is popular today, but back in the 1960s, it was widely unknown in the United States. David Ogilvie, arguably one of the most savvy advertising writers who ever lived, was assigned to promote the luxury features of the car, and devised a winning headline featuring one stunning sentence: At sixty miles an hour, the loudest sound you'll hear is the ticking of the quartz clock. Now that's a well-designed automobile!

On a somewhat smaller scale, let's consider the case of Max, a mid-sized florist who wanted to distinguish his service from those of the hundreds of other florists in his region by offering large bouquets at a fixed, reasonable price. Max bought a minute's worth of advertising on a nationally-syndicated radio talk show and sent the host a huge arrangement of flowers, followed by two attractive cards in which the florist expressed his admiration for the host and asked if he would narrate the "spot" or commercial. The pleased talk show host agreed to deliver a short pitch that sounded very much like a personal testimonial, which had an electrifying effect on the host's listening audience. Orders for fresh flowers flooded into Max's shop.

Sometimes promotion has the same effect as advertising. For example, many large companies—and quite a few small ones—make large charitable contributions in order to create a positive association, or image, of the company. In addition, the company is promoted through association with the charity. Its name can appear in association with the charity on brochures, promotional items such as T-shirts and key chains, and in broadcast media, or in whatever venue the charity is being promoted.

Too often, new entrepreneurs dismiss advertising and promotion as being too expensive or even unnecessary when they should be exploring ways to make advertising concepts work for their businesses, expanding the new customer base and luring former clients back into the fold. Advertising doesn't have to be expensive, but it pays to interview several reputable agencies to find one that is familiar with your business and compatible with your needs. Always seek out a professional agency and ensure that it takes into account the three basic rules of all communication (mentioned in my introduction) on all the work it produces for you company.

1) Know whom you want to address
2) Know what you want to say
3) Know how to convey that message effectively

What happens if these basics are ignored? I recommend that you study the rudiments of marketing and advertising methods before you contact any advertising professional or begin any campaign of your own. That way, you increase your chances of getting effective advertising tailored to marketing your product or service.

> Many entrepreneurs have been driven to bankruptcy by pouring all their assets into ill-conceived or ineffective ad campaigns or promotional efforts.

Avoiding Common Mistakes

Well, we've come to the end of my "little shop of horrors." Whether you are starting up a new business or taking over an established one, it's great to be full of enthusiasm and competitive spirit and determination. However, you can take major strides to avoid heartbreak down the road by concentrating on what *not* to do. I hope that this discussion of common errors will inspire you to avoid the many pitfalls that await the new entrepreneur.

The Spirit of Business

3

The Spirit of Business

Business should be more than a supplement to our way of life. For me, it is my way of life.
—The Author

Meaning of Spirit

There are two important elements to conducting business. The first, and best known, is the business of doing business. That involves such practical matters as setting goals, raising capital, handling accounts and developing a warrior-type attitude toward the marketplace and the competition. And we will touch upon those in later chapters.

Spirit is the second and perhaps more important aspect of business. But what is spirit? What does it mean? Why is it important? Do I have it? Where can I get it?

Spirit comes from the Latin word *spiritus*, which means "breathing" or "breath." For example, a good athletic coach "breathes" spirit in his players with his upbeat, positive spirit. "We're going to compete as hard as we can," he might tell his team before a big game. "We're going to do the best we can to win, but we're also going to play fair and square. Most important, we're going to have a lot of fun while we're doing it." If you can instill this optimistic attitude in the people who work for you, then you'll be indoctrinating them in the proper Entrepreneural Spirit.

An entrepreneur may have a vision of what could be, but if he does not possess the Spirit, he will not be able to breathe life into his dreams. They will remain bottled up in his mind, filed under the heading: *Things I Should Have Done*. And, when all is said and done, that is a sad epitaph.

Sometimes, however, Spirit is buried under negative feelings of fear, anger, frustration, disappointment, and resentment. Can you dig it out? Yes. Can you develop it? Yes. But it takes work to reclaim what is yours. I once read that for every year you carry an emotional injury, it will take two months to heal it. That too, is good news. Who doesn't have a few months or even years to give to turn their dream into a reality?

> The good news is that we all have Spirit within us.

Seven steps to Entrepreneurial Spirit

Even though we are unique individuals, we still have common threads that bind us together. Our basic commonality is our survival instinct—a more ethereal one is our need for love. We also have the need for self-expression. Of course, the depth of our need is going to determine the degree to which we fill it. For example, Jean, a very fine artist, possesses a wonderful talent for painting the beautiful flowers she grows in her garden. But the only chance you'll have to see her work is if you are invited into her home, and she offers you a cup of tea, for all her paintings are done on porcelain teacups and she has no desire to sell them.

The Spirit of Business

Jean is very content with her level of expertise. She acknowledges that she is better than most floral artists. Her satisfaction comes from knowing that she is good at what she does and appreciating that she has the time to paint flowers on teacups.

In contrast, there is Jean's friend, Barbara, who is also an artist. She is still "in search of her style," is seldom content and when she is, it isn't for long. She composes music, sings, designs jewelry, writes books and finds time to teach others various artistic skills. Her works, in all their many forms, are sold throughout the world. She feels her work is evolving and wishes that a day had more hours and the week more days.

We can always get more education, acquire more experience and enhance our natural ability. But how can we best do this? It's by unleashing our Entrepreneurial Spirit.

> Our levels of ability, education, and experience also play a major role in defining our parameters.

Each and every one of us has a different path to take to get where we are going. Even if we follow the same path we will not view our journey in the same way. The Seven Steps to Entrepreneurial Spirit is simply a guide to help you in your process of defining your entrepreneurial nature. The seven steps are:

1) Acknowledgment
2) Will
3) Desire / Passion
4) Self-evaluation
5) Patience
6) Diligence
7) Celebration

Entrepreneurship Made E-Z

Acknowledgment

I think the best place to start is always at the beginning. That way you won't miss any of the scenery and, if the need arises, you know your way back.

> To get started on the path to the Entrepreneurial Spirit, you must first acknowledge it as being real.

This is difficult for most of us because we think of reality as something that can be seen and touched. It has size, dimension and form. Spirit has none of these, but it is nonetheless real and it shows itself in the things we do. For example, let's take a look at Lawrence, a friend of mine from college. Lawrence was a terrific slalom skier, and I, like the rest of his pals, assumed that he would be a shoe-in for the winter Olympics. Unfortunately, during his Olympic trials, Lawrence took a terrible spill on the slopes. His spine was so badly injured that he was paralyzed from the waist down. Most people in this position would have been plunged into the depths of despair and never even thought about skiing again.

Not Lawrence. He had "spirit." Not only did he learn to use a special set of skis designed for paraplegics, he mastered them, and was soon skiing down the steepest and most challenging slopes in times that rivaled his old records. He actually did qualify for the Olympics—the special branch of the Olympics that features athletes with disabilities.

How did he do it? He had an indomitable spirit that refused to bow to his misfortunes. In essence, he refused to be affected by negative feelings of doubt, insecurity, failure, and gloom, and he was willing to put forth the effort to surpass his own expectations of his performance.

Lawrence's spirit was real. You could see it in the look of determination in his face before he began every run. You

The Spirit of Business

could sense it in the courage he showed every time he urged his crippled body down slopes so dangerous that experienced, "whole" skiers avoided them. Lawrence expressed his spirit through his positive emotions, his self-confidence, and his inner belief in his own innate ability to overcome hardship.

Ever wonder why alcohol is called spirits? It's because it affects our moods, our emotional balance, the essence of our being. And that's what Lawrence's spirit did. It affected his moods in a positive way, in an admirable way. All who knew him could see and appreciate his spirit as a real, valid part of this brave athlete.

The second part of acknowledging spirit is to recognize it within you. Introduce yourself to your Spirit and acknowledge its needs.

Will and Willingness

There are many meanings to the word *will*. Since you will use the word *will* in different contexts during your attempts to build up your Entrepreneurial Spirit, it's important that you understand the five ways the word is used in this book. They are as follows:

1) The facility of conscious and deliberate action
2) The power of choosing our actions
3) Volition
4) Determination
5) Disposition

The "facility of conscious and deliberate action" means freedom of will, and we are all free to do as we will. We

> Some people have a stronger "will power" than others.

also have the power to choose our actions. Fortunately, we all have the ability to strengthen our will power by making

59

Entrepreneurship Made E-Z

conscious choices that reflect a wise, careful thought process. Once we have chosen what action to take, we also have the power to assert, or exercise, our choices (volition).

We can also determine what "will be" by "willing it" to be so. It has been said that the mind is responsive to certain physical cues, such as facial expressions and spoken words. For example, psychologists sometimes counsel their depressed patients to smile even if they feel despairing, and to speak positively, no matter how they are feeling. Although this sounds simplistic, studies show that these basic measures can have a positive effect upon the moods of depressed people.

But how about the moods of undepressed entrepreneurs? Well, consider the attribute of enthusiasm for a moment. You may not jump up and down with enthusiasm about a given subject, but you know for the sake of your venture that you must muster at least a semblance of enthusiasm, just in order to get a particular job done. In essence, if you will yourself to be enthusiastic, and continue to do so, you will eventually become enthusiastic.

Willing an emotion, or even an outcome, into being does not normally happen instantaneously. Nevertheless, the true entrepreneur believes that we all have the power to will our dreams into being. That's why we so often hear the age-old warning, *Beware of what you wish for, it may come true.* And how many times have you heard someone say, "He did it by sheer will power alone"?

Now that you know you have the ability to bring about your will, it is essential that you are also aware of the disposition of your will. In other words, is it positive or negative, constructive or destructive? Productive, or out of control? My college friend Lawrence had spirit, but he also had tremendous positive will power. On the other hand, will power can be used detrimentally. For instance, the famous

The Spirit of Business

film, *Triumph of the Will*, chronicled Adolph Hitler's infamous rise to power before WWII. Just think of what he could have accomplished had he used his remarkable will power for the good of humankind. Honesty about our intent is crucial. We have the ability to hurt not only ourselves by what we will, but others as well.

Desire / Passion

People cannot make something work unless they have the desire to make it work. Desire is a deep-seated longing or craving for something that brings us satisfaction and fills us up. Passion is the term we use to measure our desires and our enthusiasm for fulfilling them. Enthusiasm, an interesting word that comes from the Greek word, *enthousiasmos*, means, "to be possessed by a god." Even the Ancients knew that great things do not happen without the desire to make them happen, and such desire seems to spring from a divine source. Desire won't flame without passion, and passion will not seize you without enthusiasm. They are inexplicably bound to each other.

As an entrepreneur, there will be times when you must persuade yourself that you are enthusiastic, even though you certainly aren't feeling that way at the moment. I have trained myself to remember the word *enthusiasm* when my *spirits* are low. It's not an immediate cure for fatigue or listlessness, but it does remind me of what got me where I am. It also reminds me that I have what it takes to accomplish my venture.

Self-Evaluation

Among all the "self" things you will have to do as an entrepreneur, here are the four most important: self-motivate, self-promote, self-praise, and self-evaluate.

> To find your Entrepreneurial Spirit, take a good look at *yourself.*

Entrepreneurship Made E-Z

More than once in this book I will refer to the need to take inventory and do an appraisal, not only of your business, but also of your physical, mental, emotional and spiritual self. One of the biggest mistakes entrepreneurs make is in not taking the time to know themselves and the tools they possess and the condition those tools are in. They somehow forget to examine their motives, review their ethics, and audit their actions.

More often than not, when an entrepreneur meets with a big failure, it is not because of some exterior entity, force, or event. It is because something within that person must be taken care of before he can achieve success. In the chapter entitled "The 12 Steps to Personal Success," I will go into much more detail about the means and methods of self-evaluation.

Diligence

Taking the path to the Entrepreneurial Spirit is like being on a diet. At the first smell of chocolate, your mouth begins to water. Next thing you know, you've eaten a candy bar, then half a cake. Hey, there's always tomorrow, right?

But what if there were no more tomorrows? What if your decisions were final? How would you feel about yourself? Would you be happy with your decisions? The effort you put into dreams? Would you be pleased about your legacy?

It is as easy to give up a business venture as it is to cast aside your latest diet plan. But the price you pay is much more than the cost of allowing yourself to forget about your business. So, during your quest for the Entrepreneurial Spirit, you must make a constant and earnest effort to find what you are looking for. You must be ever watchful and attentive to your efforts. You must painstakingly:

- Pursue
- Persist
- Persevere

The Spirit of Business

And, when you feel like giving up, pause and take a breather. Relax and remember that you have the will to accomplish your goal.

Throughout the ages, there have always been ruthless and unscrupulous business people. However, it is my contention that "honesty" and "success in business" are not irreconcilable opposites. An entrepreneur can be both honest and successful, truthful and prosperous, compassionate and commanding. (In fact, it is disheartening to think that dishonesty, deceit and a lack of compassion are the price we must pay to be successful, prosperous and commanding.) The truth is, business accomplishments can and do co-exist quite happily in the same space with out most treasured values. But we have to nurture them in ourselves. To do so, we must first rid ourselves of the "this or that," "either/or" way of thinking and start accepting that we can be both successful and ethical.

> The path of the Entrepreneurial Spirit not only makes you a better person, it also makes you better at your business.

Celebration

You don't have to reach a milestone in order to announce your satisfaction with a particular employee or client. Making a gracious, generous, or appreciative statement costs you nothing, but is worth a lot to your associates. And don't forget to congratulate yourself, at least in private.

> Finally, if you are happy in your venture and it is doing well, don't forget to celebrate.

And if you do score a significant victory—trump a competitor, sign a contract with the "perfect" client, overcome a setback, move to a new office, set up a branch location, show a substantial increase in profits—let your joy be known. Break out the champagne or the diet cola. Take your crew to lunch, or cater a small party. You work hard at making your business successful. You deserve those moments of triumph. Just be sure to share them with your hard-working staff.

The 12 Steps to Personal Success

4

The 12 Steps to Personal Success

4

To thine own self be true, and it must follow as the day the night, thou canst not prove false to any man.
—William Shakespeare, Hamlet

The Journey

The journey of an entrepreneur isn't just an external journey; it is also internal. While experience is a great teacher, it is worthless if the student has neither the ability nor willingness to integrate the lessons that experience has taught him or her and to look inward for answers.

When a leader is uncertain if he is leading his followers down the right path, he or she has to look to himself or herself for the answer. Entrepreneurs are leaders. They have a responsibility to cultivate the voice that speaks to them from deep inside. This is the voice that motivates them when others lose faith. It stirs them to action when others are content to sit on the sidelines, calls upon them to meet the challenges of change while others tremble in fear, and gives them the strength to pull creativity out of chaos while others stumble in confusion. The power to do all that is inside of you. You must develop it to its full potential if you wish to succeed as an entrepreneur.

Most of us are not born with the ability to hear and trust that innate inner voice, also called intuition. Even though we are born with it, most of us lose its clarity early, due to social conditioning, trauma, neglect, and the stultifying routine of most public schools.

In business, you will be faced with many decisions. Some of them will look good on the surface but won't feel right. Others won't look so good but will feel good. A "bad feeling" of mistrust or fear could be your intuition's way of waving a red flag concerning a certain person or project. Not to heed your own internal warning could lead to disaster. On the other hand, if your intuition gives you positive feelings about a project and you ignore those feelings and fail to act, you may be missing out on a golden opportunity.

> It is imperative that the entrepreneur learns to trust what he or she is feeling.

It is important that you trust yourself, both your logical self and your intuitive self. (And watch out, for these two will frequently contradict themselves.) To trust yourself, you will have to be scrupulously, painfully honest with yourself, and that is often not easy. We seem to have built within us a Great Deceiver that distorts the truth, juggles facts, and tries to protect us from unpleasant realities. Unfortunately, we willingly accept these distortions of reality, since that is often easier than accepting an unattractive truth about ourselves.

Take the case of Sarah, a commercial consulting artist who was undergoing a difficult period in her life at the same time that she was starting her own business. The pressure connected with her personal problems interfered

The 12 Steps to Personal Success

with her business, causing her to miss meetings, forget assignments, make mistakes in layout and execution, change copy without authorization, and in general make a very bad impression on her clientele. But throughout this period, Sarah never perceived that she was "on probation," as far as her customers were concerned. She had deceived herself into thinking that her mistakes were the fault of other people. A secretary hadn't told her about a meeting, a copywriter had told her to change the copy, a client had canceled an assignment, and so on. In fact, all the errors were Sarah's fault, but she was under so much stress that she had composed "excuses" to cover her shortcomings, and later went on to believe her own fictions. So, when her two major clients dismissed her within the same week, she was completely taken aback.

Sometimes this Deceiver works in our favor, but only for a little while. In Sarah's case, for example, her excuses at first bought her a little time in which she could have realized her deficiencies and improved her performance. Unfortunately, she didn't.

Most entrepreneurs are not looking for simple solutions. Instead they seek out the opportunity to prove or do something significant. Therefore, your quest for the truth will be a little easier but not easy. I know that my journey wasn't all smiles and level roadway. But I can say that, since a large part of my journey is behind me, I'm glad that I took the trip.

A system called Personal Mapping helped me identify the truth and adhere to reality, and I would like to share that system with you in some detail.

Personal Mapping

An entrepreneur is responsible for two types of mapping:

Entrepreneurship Made E-Z

- Business Mapping
- Personal Mapping

The more challenging one to master is Personal Mapping, which requires a twelve-step process. Personal Mapping requires trusting your intuition and being 100% honest with yourself. Self-deception will undermine all your hard work, so try to keep your Deceiver at bay.

Here are the Twelve Steps:

1) Questions
2) Answers
3) Truth
4) Honesty
5) Integrity
6) Action
7) Release
8) Forgiveness
9) Change
10) Acceptance
11) Defining Moments
12) Fast Forwarding

You will wear many hats as an entrepreneur. Some will be a good fit, but others won't. One day you will be a consultant, the next a business manager, and on the weekend you'll be a researcher scanning information on the Internet. You'll do the little things, the big things, and everything in between. However, nothing cuts deeper or stings more sharply than when you become your own psychologist, self-help guru, or whatever you wish to call yourself, as you go through your process of personal mapping.

> Each role you play is going to have some sharp edges.

The 12 Steps to Personal Success

This is not a process that you undergo once or twice during your vocation as an entrepreneur. It is an ongoing and continual process, and it is often bittersweet. I must admit there were times when I would tire of the procedure and think of taking up another career. Why? Because I wanted it to be right. Every time I uncovered or discovered something new about myself, I also uncovered new questions about myself that had to be asked and answered. Often the questions were hard and involved a lot of soul-searching, some of it not very pleasant. Sometimes the answers I unearthed were not very flattering either. True, yes, but attractive, no.

> No one likes to admit and confront the fact that he or she can be selfish, conceited, stubborn or gullible under certain conditions, but those admissions are the first steps to overcoming negative thoughts and behavior.

Let's examine each step to Personal Mapping, one at a time. The first is:

Questions

Asking questions is a great way to find out information. It is also a sign of intelligence. That's a good thing to know, because personal mapping can't work unless you ask questions. The more you ask, the more information you will obtain, and the less need you'll have to ask questions. The key here is to ask yourself the questions—then answer them yourself.

Answers

In the context of Personal Mapping, we are going to view an answer as a solution to a problem. That solution will require you to be held answerable for the problem in the first place. You are expected to get a full accounting of the problem and the solution, and to accept responsibility for both.

Once you have asked yourself questions, you must listen carefully to your own answers and what they are trying to tell you. Where are they coming from? Do they seem logical? Or intuitive? Don't be surprised if the answer to your question comes back as another question. Sometimes we have to increase our store of experience and knowledge before we are ready to receive an answer. For example, I once asked myself for permission to begin a new project that seemed to have a high level of risk attached to it. The answer I found within myself was, "Why did you wait so long to begin?"

Other times, the answer just isn't clear, or will seem to be the answer to an entirely different question. I've noticed that, when I understand an answer, there is no point in asking the question again for clarification. I'll just receive the same mysterious answer, or be reminded that answers don't always come right away. They could take years to present themselves. Don't worry. When you least expect it, your answer will arrive in the nick of time. (Like actors, answers seem to be like dramatic entrances.)

Sometimes answers are symbolic, and sometimes embedded in a memory of childhood, or in the lyrics of a song. Perhaps the answer will be as elusive as a feeling

> Keep in mind that answers rarely take the form of clear, concise instructions in a well-written service manual.

that descends upon you suddenly and overwhelms you. Whatever form the answer takes, make sure that you are listening for it and that you recognize it when it appears.

For Charles William Post, the founder of what became General Foods, the answer to his dreams came at breakfast. A salesman for an agricultural equipment company, Post's

The 12 Steps to Personal Success

business ventures drained his health and his pocketbook, and in 1891 he was admitted to the Battle Creek Sanitarium run by Dr. John H. Kellogg. Post was at the end of his rope mentally and emotionally, but one small thing brightened his day—a caramel-flavored cereal drink that Kellogg had invented. After he had recovered some of his health, Post, inspired by Kellogg, set out to invent his own breakfast foods. Experimentation and a series of rejections and successes led to the formulation of Grape-Nuts Cereal and later, Post Toasties, both of which are consumer favorites today. It's hard to believe that a breakfast drink inspired a reversal of fortune for this burned-out hardware salesman, but that's just what happened. Post had the presence of mind to realize his answer when he saw it and the courage to capitalize on it.

One of the toughest answers comes from asking this question:

Do I like the way I see myself?

If you don't, you will have to ask yourself why, so stay on the lookout for answers. Eventually, you'll be required to make changes in your behavior or perceptions, but change will come after you confront some of the following issues.

Truth

For centuries, philosophers, scientists, and poets have been trying to define or at least understand just what *truth* is, or if it exists at all. We often define truth as consisting of facts, but facts only refer to what we think is true at any one time. For instance, in the late 1800s, a huge stone head stood in the desert in Egypt next to the Great Pyramid of Cheops. You could go to Egypt and see that stone head. You could touch it. It was a tangible *fact* that the statue of a human head existed in that location. However, when the sand under the head was excavated, a new fact emerged. The stone head

•

was attached to a stone body, a lion's body. Now the "facts" about the Sphinx had changed, and the *true* nature of the statue was revealed. As this true story indicates, facts are transitory, but the truth is more enduring. The difficulty comes in trying to pin down the truth.

To get as close to the truth as they can, entrepreneurs gather factual, reliable information about topics that impact their business. They don't approach a new project blindly. They know that a certain amount of risk accompanies every business venture. The entrepreneur who waltzes into an existing business without researching it first, without looking at the numbers, without—as far as is possible—establishing the truth behind that business' potential for success and the nature of the competition is sure to fail.

> Like scientists and poets, entrepreneurs are truth seekers.

Truth also applies to ourselves, our very natures, our most deeply guarded personality traits. The dedicated entrepreneur will not shy away from his own failings, or his strong points, but try to find ways to use both to his advantage. Look at the acting career of W.C. Fields, a mediocre vaudeville entertainer who took advantage of his very real irascible personality to create one of the world's most engaging, unforgettable screen personas. Imagine the results if Fields had tried to mask his natural tendencies in his hilarious films.

Remember the quotation from *Hamlet* at the beginning of this chapter? "To thine own self be true, then it must follow as the day the night, thou canst not prove false to any man." You, more than anyone else, know intuitively

> Rely upon your powers of intuition to identify and recognize your own strengths and weaknesses.

what is right and wrong for yourself, what is a good choice, a disastrous choice, or a gamble. Your intellect will not always be able to steer you in the direction of the "truth" about your nature. As Shakespeare suggests, if you know the truth about yourself, you're less likely to try to deceive others. One tool that can help you "be true" to yourself is honesty, truth's handmaiden.

Honesty

We live in an interesting society. On one hand, we are taught that honesty is the best policy. Then we learn that complete disclosure in social situations is not appreciated at all. We don't tell people they have gained weight or look old in order to show our own powers of observation Part of common courtesy is learning when not to say something, even if it is the truth..

Remember a certain toothpaste whose advertising promised to make your teeth whiter and your breath fresher and, as a result, would make you instantly alluring to the best-looking members of the opposite sex? Did the toothpaste work? No? So much for honesty in advertising. Advertisers are far more concerned with creating an image than in promulgating the truth. (In this case the truth is, "Buy this toothpaste. It will reduce the incidence of cavities a little for you and will make money for us.")

However, as an author and businessman with a strong belief in advertising, I can assure you that ads like this are very rarely seen anymore. The content of most advertising is so highly scrutinized by the media as well as the attorneys from both the advertiser and the agency (both of whom are liable) that untruthful advertising is now mostly a thing of the past.

While it may appear that we only give lip service to the virtues of honesty, that is no excuse not to strive to be truthful with yourself. Your ultimate success is going to depend upon just how honest you are about your

> If there is any situation in which to be honest it is with yourself.

needs, strengths, weaknesses and abilities. By being honest, you will have laid a very strong foundation that will serve you well as both an entrepreneur and a person.

But what does it really mean to be honest? It's more than merely being truthful, that is, revealing facts as we understand them. When you are honest, you are honorable in your principles, intentions, and actions. You are not disposed to lie, cheat, mislead, or steal. You are upright, fair, frank and genuine, and can be trusted to follow up on your promises. You gain credence and respect from your peers. You are consistent in the standards that you set for yourself, both in business and your personal life.

Your Personal Mapping will be a lot more effective if you are honest with yourself. Your ultimate success will depend upon just how honest you are about your needs, strengths, weaknesses and abilities, both with yourself and with others. Invariably, when we try to fool others, we end up hurting no one but ourselves.

We are all familiar with athletes and entertainers who convince themselves that they have not lost their skills or abilities and continue to perform well past the time they should retire. Not only are the results often embarrassing, but very often they can be physically disastrous. Sometimes, the motivation is financial, but more often it is the failure of the performers to be truly honest with themselves.

When it comes down to brass tacks, we are not how we think we are, but how we conduct ourselves in everything we do. And if we act honestly and without deception, we'll be taking giant steps toward personal integrity.

The 12 Steps to Personal Success

Integrity

Being honest with yourself is essential in developing your integrity, which is a measure of your adherence to moral and ethical principals. Contrary to popular opinion, being an entrepreneur does not exempt you from morals and ethics. "It's nothing personal—it's only business," is *not* the motto of the successful entrepreneur. It's the motto of the weasel who cheats his way to the top before falling all the way to the bottom.

Integrity, morals and ethics are essential to the successful entrepreneur, that is, the businessperson who turns a profit. Why? Because they are the basis upon which people determine many of their product choices. They would rather do business with someone they can trust than with the weasel who smiles all the way up to the point before he bites you. Also, honesty and integrity lead to credibility, which is essential in the quest to attract dependable investors.

Action

Entrepreneurs often possess the ability to see those things that may come into being. But not all visionaries are entrepreneurs. To be an entrepreneur, you must *act*, not only upon your ideas, but

> Entrepreneurs are usually visionaries.

upon the truth of what you have discovered about yourself. An entrepreneur will act because he has a deep-seated, personal drive or need to build something new, different, or better, regardless of what other people may think or say. An entrepreneur sees competition as a challenge, and likes nothing better than to improve upon an existing product or service, or better yet, to come up with some thrilling innovation. An entrepreneur thrives on action, and when that is combined with change, something remarkable happens.

Action + Change = Opportunity

> To a true entrepreneur, few things are more important than the opportunity to grow and succeed.

Of course, to make his opportunity work, the entrepreneur will have to act upon it wisely and creatively, since any opportunity is only as good as its execution. But before he or she can take advantage of that opportunity, he or she will have to forgive himself or herself for his or her failures in the past, times when he or she either let opportunity slip through his or her fingers, or strangled a great concept with a poor execution.

Release

To release something is not just a matter of freeing it from confinement or obligation. It also means relinquishing or surrendering yourself to something or someone. In doing your Personal Mapping, you will be doing both activities. As you uncover hidden aspects of yourself that are new to you, you'll be setting that part of you free so you can benefit from it. You'll also be letting go of old things you don't need anymore—rigid thought patterns, detrimental emotional points of view, outdated beliefs, flawed concepts, and narrow ideas. At the same time, you'll discover innate personal traits that define who you are, and you must acknowledge them and surrender yourself to them. Even a negative trait, like a hair-trigger temper, is part of you and helps define who you are. Of course, all of this freeing and surrendering is easier said than done.

Often, it takes a dramatic change in circumstances to find out about our hidden character and capabilities. That was very much the case with the 33rd President of the United States Harry Truman.

The 12 Steps to Personal Success

Selected as a vice-presidential running mate for Franklin Roosevelt in what was Roosevelt's unprecedented fourth term of office, he was overwhelmingly elected. An examination of his background would lead to the conclusion that his selection by the President had more to do with gathering votes and obligations to the Democratic Party than his history or abilities.

Truman who did not finish college was a bank clerk, farmer, soldier, businessman (a partner in a men's haberdashery store), and a senator from Missouri. When Roosevelt died, he was suddenly and dramatically put in the most powerful position on earth. He responded by winning an upset election over a heavily favored Thomas Dewey and then being re-elected for a second term. During his tenure, he made the decision to drop the atomic bomb, presided over the Korean war, approved the creation of NATO, and is now considered one of our most effective past presidents.

Early in my own career, I was associated with a man who was very successful in building a large company. In those days, going public was something of a novelty, and he knew a great deal about how to go public. However, as his company grew, I noticed many "holes" in his organization, and I finally realized why. He had a basic management flaw: paternalism. This man felt obligated to be a sort of "godfather" to all of his employees and keep them all employed, regardless of whether or not they could do their work effectively. If they couldn't do a certain task, he would shift them into less stressful positions, then undertake their responsibilities in addition to his own.

I met with this man many years later on an airplane and talked to him about why his company collapsed. He attributed the failure to various facts and figures that had nothing to do with the real reason. Amazingly, he didn't seem to realize his problem, even in hindsight. I gently pointed out that because of his management decisions, the executives who worked under him never really achieved any substantial success. He agreed, and admitted that, because he had surrounded himself with people who lacked talent and ambition, he had in fact been a major contributor to his own downfall in business.

On the plus side of the ledger is the story of Jack Welch, the former chairman of General Electric, probably one of the most successful and renowned business managers of our time. When asked how he spent his time, he replied that he spent about 75% in evaluating, motivating, rewarding, and encouraging personnel. Welch used what is called the 20-70-10% rule. He tried to make sure that the 20% who produced results at a high level continued to produce, and that the 70% who did not produce as well had an incentive to improve. The 10% who did very little constructive work, regardless of incentives, were reviewed or terminated so that they could seek other, more suitable occupations. This last task wasn't easy for Welch, but he did it in order to preserve the viability of the company. The historic, ongoing success of General Electric speaks for itself.

Don't be afraid of jettisoning anything that is holding you back. Chances are, it is repressing something positive and creative inside you which only needs the sunlight in order to blossom.

Forgiveness

Most people find that it is easier to forgive someone else than it is to forgive themselves. Forgiving another

> Forgiveness is the ability to grant a pardon for an offense or wrongdoing.

person places you in a position of kindness or power. Forgiving yourself places you in a position of admitting that you have erred. I think entrepreneurs find it especially hard to forgive themselves for two reasons:

The 12 Steps to Personal Success

- They love to be in positions that demand responsibility.
- They expect and demand more of themselves than others expect of themselves.

If there is a problem to be solved or fixed, entrepreneurs do it. They are normally very competent at doing this when it comes to the external aspects of operating their enterprise—planning, hiring, scheduling, and so on. But remember, business is not just external. It is also internal.

Throughout the process of Personal Mapping, you will find not only new areas of yourself that need to be adjusted, defined, changed, or accepted, but also some "old business" you thought was finished but wasn't. Perhaps you never really forgave yourself for "exaggerating" your experience on your resume or crushing a former friend who had become a competitor. When your old faults surface, try not to be hard on yourself.

It's important to remember that entrepreneurs are truly special people. They:

- Work harder than most
- Think outside the box
- Appreciate the efforts of others
- Are generous to their community
- Are fierce fighters
- Ignore idle chatter and gossip

Make an effort to recall all these good points about yourself as you go through the process of Personal Mapping in your search for the Entrepreneurial Spirit. Forgive yourself for your weaknesses, your wrongdoings, the things you should be and aren't, and for what you are and don't want to be. In other words, be kind to yourself when you make a mistake. The best quarterbacks in football are the ones who can throw an interception, forget about it, and come back to lead their team to victory.

> Personal problems cannot be fixed without forgiveness.

Take Clifford, for example, not a quarterback, but an older businessman who has a special ritual. He leaves work early every Wednesday to bowl a frame or two at a local alley. Once, when I asked him why he did this, Clifford smiled sadly. "My son David had Down's Syndrome, and the only sporting activity he could do was bowling. He loved it. On the first Wednesday of every month, the special club he belonged to would rent part of an alley and he and his friends would go bumper bowling. He begged me to join him, but I just didn't have the time. At least, that's what I thought back then. When he died ten years ago, I thought my heart would break. I couldn't forgive myself for putting my business first, before my son. Then a friend told me, 'It's not too late. Go bowling now.' So I did, and you know, it helps. I can feel David's excitement whenever I get a strike. By taking the time out now to remember him, I've managed to forgive myself."

Change

> To change is to become different.

Now that we've laid the groundwork, we can talk about change. Nothing ever stays the same. It's true. You only have to look around you to see for yourself. The changes in the seasons, the changes in your infant daughter as she grows up, the changes in your marketing plan when your inexperienced associate gets hold of it. If something did manage to stay the same, it would be in violation of the rules of physics.

A dear friend of mine told me that, as a child, she could look out the window of her parents' home in Portland, Oregon and get a clear view of Mt. St. Helens. The sight of

The 12 Steps to Personal Success

the massive, snow-capped mountain, glimmering pink in the sunset like a giant, inverted sugar cone, gave her a feeling of permanence and comfort. "I thought that surely here was one huge thing that would never change, at least in my lifetime." My friend laughed. "Bzzzt!" she said, imitating a game show sound effect. "Wrong! Ten years later, St. Helens blew its top and turned into a very large soup tureen. That's when I learned Rule Number One of the universe: Change is inevitable."

Change demands energy. The energy you exert is in direct proportion to how much change is needed. Putting a new coat of paint on your living room walls is easier than building on a two-story addition. Sometimes all you need is a fresh coat of paint. Other times, you'll need to get out the lumber, hammers, saws, nails and hire a couple of professional construction workers to help you out. Unfortunately, you can't just throw money at a builder and walk away. You are the builder. Nevertheless, being in charge isn't the same as being alone. Don't make the mistake of thinking that they are one and the same. If you think you're alone, you will be.

Now, during periods of change, there will be times when you feel alone, even miserably alone. You'll feel as if you are the only person who is being required to go through the changing process. I've spoken to several entrepreneurs who have started companies, and each one said that they thought he or she was the only person in the world who was undergoing the blues and insecurities that haunt new founders. Of course, all of these men and women felt almost the same way.

Self-fulfilling prophecies do happen, and if you think something is true, it tends to become real for you. This is great if you think of yourself as a successful entrepreneur, but it can also cause self-pity, depression and anger. These problems can all be avoided if you are aware of the nature

Entrepreneurship Made E-Z

> Whatever door you walk through, you must realize that you are not the first person to do so.

of change and how it touches everyone. If a situation is new to you, particularly a distressing situation, remember that others have passed through the same way. Seek them out for advice and solace. There are very few situations in which I would advise you to go solo. Dealing with the aches and pains of change isn't one of them.

Acceptance

When you accept something, you take what has been offered. Normally, you accept something because you find it favorable, or at least satisfactory or adequate, such as a business deal that has been negotiated between you and a competitor. Or, you might accept something that you believe to be true or sound. For instance, most Americans accept the idea that our country was founded on the principles of justice and personal freedom. Or, acceptance might mean that you have taken on certain responsibilities or duties, such as a person accepting the position of CEO, or a grown child accepting his responsibilities toward his aging parents.

All three definitions apply in Personal Mapping. You accept something because you:

- Find it agreeable
- Believe it to be true
- Take responsibility for it

All three of these definitions can apply to a personal experience. Many years ago, I was a partner in luxury real estate development. The financing for this project consisted of raising money from a group of investors for a limited partnership (of which I was one of the two general partners) and securing a substantial land acquisition and construction loan from a major financial institution.

The 12 Steps to Personal Success

Unfortunately, because of a combination of bad timing, poor product acceptance, and delays in getting to market (in other words, it took too long, cost too much, and sold too slowly) the lenders became disenchanted and wanted us to turn the property over to a local high-rise developer. Although the prospect was not pleasant, it was agreed to, and I believed it was truly the best solution. I took responsibility for making it happen.

There were, however, several problems. The property had to be turned over free and clear. There were four families living there, and two contracts for purchase. I had to find a way to return some money to our investors, and there was a loan from a local bank guaranteed by both general partners. After several months of nervewracking and exhausting negotiations with the various parties, I was fortunate to achieve all the desired objectives. The property was sold to the lender's nominee, the individual investors received enough cash to make them whole, and the bank was repaid. The owners of the houses on this property and those who had signed contracts were satisfied, and the financial institution was pleased with the net results.

Although the results of this building project were terribly disappointing, both the investors and the financial institutions were so pleased with our not walking away from the problems that may of the same people invested in my subsequent ventures.

In my own case, accepting and embracing the concept of Personal Mapping as a daily part of my routine made a tremendous difference in my life. I found that it kept me focused and clear about my intent. At some point, and I'm not certain when it happened, taking part in Personal Mapping became like opening a birthday gift. In every "package" I unwrapped I found a surprise, a treasure. Well, sometimes they were treasures I didn't want or need anymore, but I accepted them anyway. I accepted the fact

85

that sometimes I could be too passive or slow to take advantage of a situation and other "gifts" that gave me useful, if painfully honest, information about myself.

> Through Personal Mapping, I eventually became more and more aware of my own talents and weaknesses.

The gifts I received from Personal Mapping played a big part in my decision to take the leap from being an intrapreneur—an executive for someone else's company—to being an entrepreneur.

In the next section, you'll read about a difficult time in my life in which I had very mixed feelings regarding acceptance. On one hand, I accepted a task that I believed was truly vital for the health of the company I worked for, and I accepted responsibility for getting the job done, which I did. This part of the task was agreeable and personally rewarding. On the other hand, I soon discovered that even the greatest accomplishment loses much of its pleasure if it is made for a company that doesn't belong to you. And this lesson was hard for me to accept.

Defining Moments

A defining moment is a point at which the essential nature of your character, another's character, a situation, or a group is revealed and defined. We often reach a point in our interactions with another individual when that person's true intent becomes crystal clear, and we suddenly discover a parcel of truth.

> Defining moments can be positive, negative, or cause a combination of positive and negative feelings.

Accepting the moment of discovery, especially a negative discovery, may be difficult at first because you may feel disappointed or let down. Something you had accepted as a truth has been revealed as a

The 12 Steps to Personal Success

charade. Perhaps a person you trusted has proven to be unworthy of your trust. Or perhaps something you believed about yourself as the truth has been negated. This is an unsettling experience.

When you undergo your own defining moment, you may experience a glut of emotions—shock, disbelief, anger, frustration, confusion. But, mixed in with all of those volatile emotions will be something very exhilarating—a sense of resolve and peace. Defining moments reveal the truth about what kind of person you really are. I am not saying you will like what you discover, but at least you will know what you are dealing with.

My defining moment changed the course of my life. I was president of a large company that had decided to purchase a major casino that later became a chain of casinos. The purchase was difficult, because financing for casinos was extremely difficult to obtain at the time. The Chairman of the Board of the company, by the way, had given me full responsibility to procure the financing, as he was both unavailable and unwilling to do it.

After many challenges, I managed to raise the nearly $60 million needed for the purchase, which gave me a tremendous amount of personal satisfaction. However, on the day of the closing, guess who got all the credit for acquiring the casino? Guess who signed all the papers? Yes, it was the Chairman of the Board, not me. At that moment, I realized that I would never be able to achieve true self-satisfaction and a sense of well-being unless I achieved success for a company of my own. Later, after establishing Transmedia, I discovered that I derived far more satisfaction from "being my own boss" and living in my own store than from any of the luxury perks or lavish expense accounts that I received from my prior positions working for other people.

Fast Forwarding

This is a fun part of Personal Mapping. In fast forwarding, you get to be the hero of your own story. I find that the easiest way to go about this is to physically draw yourself a map so that you may refer to it whenever you wish. So get yourself a pen and paper: You're going to draw your own map. First you have to ask yourself the question: *Where am I now?* Mark the spot with an X as your starting point. Next ask yourself: *Where do I want to go?* Mark it on your map as your final destination. Then:

Take Inventory:
- What do you need?
- What do you already have?
- Where will you get what you need?

Chart the Course:
- How will I get there?
- Measure the distance: How long is the journey?

Timeline:
- How long will it take to get from one mile marker to another?
- When will I get to my destination?
- How much time do I have?
- How much time am I willing to give?

Write it all down. Frame it and put it on a wall, if that is what it takes to keep you focused and aware of your future. Your map will change a dozen times or more as you explore territory that is new to you. Remember, at any time you may wish to stop to ask directions from someone who has been there before. I warn you that you are going to be in for some remarkable stories. Learn from them.

The 12 Steps to Personal Success

As an entrepreneur, you'll always be embarking on a new venture which will also be a new adventure. That is your nature. If you fail at one thing, it will be at successfully suppressing your Entrepreneurial Spirit.

> Personal mapping helps you develop insights and teaches you to trust your intuition which should be the determining factor in any venture.

Return to Change

Once you have gone through the steps of Personal Mapping, the end result is change. Sometimes it is only a better understanding of why you do what you do. Sometimes it is more profound, and you will discover something about yourself that leads you to a whole new life. Whatever, however, whenever doesn't matter. The point is that you are growing and changing and moving in the right direction.

What Is Your Entrepreneurial Potential?

5

What Is Your Entrepreneurial Potential? 5

Take the following exam.

Before you begin to panic as visions of that dreaded Calculus 101 final exam assault your memory, relax. This test will not be graded by anyone but you. Nor will it mean anything to anyone but you, nor be used by anyone but you. There is no pass or fail, right or wrong, no A, B, C, D, or F grades. So why take it? The intent of this test is not so much to evaluate you or your skills but to help you discover important aspects of your personality, as they pertain to being or becoming an entrepreneur.

Understand that there are many different varieties, and levels, of entrepreneurship. Some people will always choose the "high risk" answer, some will choose the "low risk" answer, and many will range all over the map. No matter how you answer,

> In your career as an entrepreneur, a mixture of high risks in some areas and lower risks in others will help provide the overall balance you need to become a success.

you could still be perfectly suited to going into business for yourself. Hopefully, this test will help you determine the right mixture of risk for you

Entrepreneurship Made E-Z

For the first 14 statements in this list, simply check off the choice that best describes how much you agree with each statement. For example, if the statement is, "I consider myself resilient," choose *True* if you agree, (Yes, I am definitely resilient), or *False* if you disagree (No, I am not very resilient.). If you believe that the statement describes your thoughts and actions at least 51% of the time, choose *More True than False*. If you believe that the statement is partially true but describes your thoughts and actions less than 51% of the time, choose *More False than True*. Item 15 is a short essay question.

So, what are you waiting for? Let's find out more about your entrepreneurial potential.

Test Statements

1) I consider myself a leader.

    ○ True
    ○ False
    ○ More True than False
    ○ More False than True

2) I have the ability to inspire others to believe in me.

    ○ True
    ○ False
    ○ More True than False
    ○ More False than True

3) When I believe that I am right, I have the self-confidence to persist until I get the job done.

    ○ True
    ○ False
    ○ More True than False
    ○ More False than True

What Is Your Entrepreneural Potential?

4) We have little control over what happens to us.

   - ○ True
   - ○ False
   - ○ More True than False
   - ○ More False than True

5) I am more frightened by the thought of losing than I am thrilled by the excitement of winning.

   - ○ True
   - ○ False
   - ○ More True than False
   - ○ More False than True

6) I avoid confrontation whenever possible.

   - ○ True
   - ○ False
   - ○ More True than False
   - ○ More False than True

7) I find small details bothersome and refuse to deal with them.

   - ○ True
   - ○ False
   - ○ More True than False
   - ○ More False than True

8) When I make a mistake, I can easily forgive myself and move on.

   - ○ True
   - ○ False
   - ○ More True than False
   - ○ More False than True

Entrepreneurship Made E-Z

9) I never take myself so seriously that I lose my ability to laugh at myself.

   ○ True
   ○ False
   ○ More True than False
   ○ More False than True

10) I am able to work long hours alone when required to do so.

    ○ True
    ○ False
    ○ More True than False
    ○ More False than True

11) I have something valuable to contribute to society.

    ○ True
    ○ False
    ○ More True than False
    ○ More False than True

12) I welcome change.

    ○ True
    ○ False
    ○ More True than False
    ○ More False than True

13) I can plan for the future and still take care of day-to-day activities.

    ○ True
    ○ False
    ○ More True than False
    ○ More False than True

What Is Your Entrepreneural Potential?

14) I am good at setting priorities.
    - ○ True
    - ○ False
    - ○ More True than False
    - ○ More False than True

15) Imagine that you are at a convention geared to your industry. You are either:

    a) a major executive of a large company, hosting a hospitality room for all the representatives from various smaller companies with whom you do business, or

    b) the owner of one of these small companies.

    Which position would you prefer to hold? Why?

Do You Have Leadership Potential?

6

Do You Have Leadership Potential?

Remember, there's no right or wrong.

So, how do you think you fared? We'll soon find out! For the sake of convenience and ease of presentation, I have broken the answer section into three separate chapters, each addressing five different statements. Following is a key to understanding your responses to the statements in the exam. Note that the responses include an assessment of the level of risk indicated by each answer.

a) **High Risk**—indicates that you will take the greatest level of risk.

b) **Moderate Risk**—indicates an intermediate level of risk.

c) **Low Risk**—indicates the lowest level of risk.

d) **Combination**—indicates a wide range of risk

For example, if you chose a High Risk response for the statement, "I consider myself resilient," it means that you are probably willing to take substantial risks because you are highly flexible, not easily discouraged, and expect to bounce back after a loss. A Moderate Risk response means that you are reasonably flexible and would probably assume a significant risk, but only in certain areas or under certain conditions. A Low Risk response indicates that you are conservative in this area and would not count on your resilience to help you recover after a loss. You would prefer to avoid the risk in the first place. Your choice might also indicate a wide range of risk, from a moderate to high level of risk, or low to moderate, or even low to high.

See the end of Chapter Eleven for an analysis of your risk-taking potential, based in part upon your responses to the statements in the test.

Statement One:

I consider myself a leader.

a) True—High Risk

You're the alpha male or female entrepreneur who puts yourself on the front lines. The buck stops with you. You're more than willing to take on all the responsibility for the success of your project, and, in fact, have to struggle with yourself in order to delegate tasks. People look to you for direction, and you are happy to provide it.

> Just be careful not to let your ego become so inflated that you cannot learn from others and admit when you are wrong.

You are goal-oriented and driven by a need to compete and a desire to succeed. You both seek your own solutions to problems and solicit solutions from others. You'll gladly accept a fairly high degree of risk if the rewards are great enough, for you have the self-confidence a true leader needs to succeed. In fact, you are happiest when taking on the greatest challenges. Your motto is, "Nothing ventured, nothing gained. Follow me."

b) False—Low Risk

You're not a leader, you're a follower, and you know it. You're happy to go after the low-hanging fruit and not reach for the big, shiny apples way at the top of the tree. You strive for success, but in small ways that are easier to achieve. Maybe you're an "intrepraneur" working for a large company that is headed by a hard-changing entrepreneur. You make many decisions and take some risks, but most of the rewards for your hard work go to someone else. Your motto is "The officer leading the charge is the first to get shot."

c) More True than False—Moderate Risk

You lead, but not everyone follows. If you have a business partner, chances are the two of you have a lot of disagreements. You tend to avoid the projects with the highest risk, instinctively knowing that you probably don't have the flexibility, determination or charisma needed to see such a difficult task through to completion. You could achieve success in business, but probably not at the highest level. Your motto is, "Give it the old college try!"

d) More False than True—Moderate Risk

You're a follower up to a point, but if you see incompetence, rigidity, or indecision in your leader, you just might try to replace him or, more likely, start off on your own. In order for you to lead and take a risk, a project will have to appeal to you personally and have a fairly good chance of success. Like the "b" person, the call of the wild risk does nothing for you. You'd prefer not to stick your neck out unless you feel you must. Your motto is, "Take the bull by the horns, but only when you have to."

Statement Two:

I have the ability to inspire others to believe in me.

a) True—High Risk

Like the leaders in (a) of Question 1, you have faith in yourself, your beliefs, and your decisions. You may not consider yourself a leader, but you are self-confident and desire success, not only for yourself but for those who help you and support you. You are willing to risk more because, in part, you wish to reward and impress those who believe in you. You could be a teacher or a minister, perhaps not literally but figuratively, showing others the way to success and leading by example. Chances are you are someone's mentor, or long to be one. If you have the ability to inspire others, your task as an entrepreneur is a lot easier, since you'll be more likely to be able to persuade people of the merits of your product or service, and therefore be able to attract and inspire investors and shareholders. Your motto is, "My teammates and I are going to the Superbowl! And we're gonna win!"

b) False—Low to Moderate Risk

You're a lone wolf, a go-it-alone sort of person. You may be dedicated, talented, and self-assured, but achieving a high level of success will be an uphill battle for you, even if you've got a stellar product. You're not likely to take the greater risks because you suspect, like Eeyore the donkey, that no one is going to go along with your brilliant agenda or share your outstanding ideas.

Entrepreneurs don't necessarily need a support staff, at least not in the beginning, but they do need to be able to exude trustworthiness and dependability. Can you do this? Or are you so introspective that others misinterpret your intentions? Even the greatest entrepreneurs surround themselves with a skilled, highly motivated

Do You Have Leadership Potential?

staff. The famous industrialist Andrew Carnegie said it best when he confessed that his true strength was the ability to surround himself with people who were brighter than he was. Your motto is, "I did it my way."

c) More True than False—Moderate Risk

The vast majority of low-to-medium successful entrepreneurs are in this category and the next. Of course, in the world of the entrepreneur, chance plays a big role. Sometimes the spoils go to the person who wins the trust of a key player in an industry or enterprise, and that's all it takes to secure success. I'm reminded of the humble

> Entrepreneurs either inspire a relatively small number of followers and backers, or they have only a portion of these people's support and trust.

beginnings of Stephen Spielberg, who once, in his youth, struck out on his own during a guided tour of a Hollywood studio. Though a trespasser, he caught the interest of a producer, who took him under his wing for the rest of the day and gave the 14-year-old Spielberg a studio pass, allowing him free entry to the lot any day he wished. The rest is history, of course, but inspiring trust in just that one influential person paid off handsomely for the talented moviemaker. Your motto is, "Give me a lever long enough and a fulcrum strong enough and I can move the world."

d) More False than True—Moderate Risk

Not a complete isolationist like (b), you nevertheless gravitate toward being on your own. You may be highly motivated yourself, but motivating others isn't high on your list, nor is it your strongest attribute. You are confident about yourself and your abilties, but you generally don't work well with employees. You probably own your own business, and perhaps even employ a single, trusted assistant. Perhaps you are a salesperson working on commission only, like an insurance agent. Your motto is, "Damn the torpedoes. I'm going in alone!"

Statement Three:

When I believe that I am right, I have the self-confidence to persist until I get the job done.

a) True—High Risk

Nothing can sink an enterprise quicker than self-doubt. Fortunately, you don't have any. Your success in any project depends upon your commitment to the project, and you won't become fully committed unless and until you know that you are in the right. When you reach that stage, your very strong belief in yourself takes over, and in essence, you and the project are one. It is a challenge that you must see through to completion, for your own sake. Like Christopher Columbus, you're willing to sail on the most dangerous seas—and you probably will—because you know the earth is round. People in authority admire that depth of commitment, courage and persistence, and they'll reward you for it with their support.

Take note, however: No matter how deep your commitment, it is important that you have the good sense to be impartial and to realize when a project will never succeed, no matter how hard you try. At that point, you must be courageous enough to abandon the project. This won't be easy for you, so be forewarned.

Also, your intense level of belief and persistence may be hard on your family. When you are wedded to a project this deeply, other ties are often strained, or even sacrificed. But that's the level of commitment that is usually necessary for the highest level of entrepreneurial success. Your motto is, "Hell will freeze over before I give up!"

b) False—Low Risk

Commitment and "being right" just aren't all that important to you. While you may be fairly self-confident, your self-confidence is not bound to proving yourself or persisting in the long haul. You are not motivated by challenges, but rather by whatever rewards the project offers. You'll assign a certain amount of time, effort or money to a project, and if it doesn't bear fruit within the scope of those limitations, you'll move on to the next, or at least start looking for a new, less resistant project. As a result of focusing upon the end rewards instead of seeing something through to the end, you aren't willing to take on a high, or even moderate level of risk. You'll give something a try—usually one try—and if it doesn't work out, you assume that "it wasn't meant to be." Your motto is, "Que sera, sera."

c) More True than False—Moderate Risk

You believe in the old saying, "Nothing ventured, nothing gained." You're just not sure how much you want to venture. Unlike (a) above, you're not likely to bet the family farm on a project, even if you are convinced that you are right. The truth is that, even when you think you are right, there is often a nagging doubt that keeps you from committing 100% of your heart, mind and soul to any enterprise. How many times have you walked up to the edge of the precipice, but did not have the faith in yourself, your associates and your project to take that step into thin air and allow your faith to support you? At the end of the day, after a long, comfortable life, you might be chastising yourself for not pushing a little harder, for taking that final step. Your motto is, "Since you can't foresee the future, stop while you're ahead."

Entrepreneurship Made E-Z

d) More False than True—Low to Moderate Risk

You're not nibbling all the goodies in the Chocolate Box of Life, but you've been tempted, and perhaps even given in several times. You might have started a project with enthusiasm and even convinced yourself that you were committed to it, but when the going got hard, you doubted yourself and began looking for ways to gracefully back out. You've never had a complete failure, but you're not likely to achieve a high degree of success either, unless you are at exactly the right place at the right time, and that amounts to luck. On the other hand, if you find a project that you truly can commit to, heart and soul, you might be able to summon the inner strength to see you through to the end. Your motto is, "I love you, but if it doesn't work out, we can get a divorce."

Statement Four:

We have little control over what happens to us.

a) True—High Risk

My friend, you are a fatalist. Marooned on an island with Robinson Crusoe, you'd probably be sitting on the shore, bemoaning your fate, while he built a hut and tamed wild goats. Sometimes realizing that our control over certain situations is marginal at best is a good thing—it ensures that you aren't likely to waste years and years on impractical projects. Your key at succeeding is to use the "little control" you believe you have to shape events to your benefit. The problem is that, when you experience any sort of resistance, you're likely to raise your arms in defeat and cry out, "Fate had decreed my failure!" Hence

> Although fatalists don't usually make the best entrepreneurs, fatalism doesn't write you off the E-list completely.

Do You Have Leadership Potential?

you assume the lowest risks possible, and eke out minor successes. When your competitor eats your lunch, you shake your head, knowing that forces greater than you are at work. The trouble is, the greater force in this case is your competitor and his dogged sense of determination. Someone is going to succeed, Mr. and Ms. Fatalist—that's destiny. Why can't it be you? Your motto is, "I tried, but the Fates were against me."

b) False—Low Risk

You, like the fatalist's competitor in the example above, believe that men and women have free will, which makes them free to steer their own course in life and become master of their own fates. And if your book of life already is written down, so be it. There's no harm in trying to make revisions. You rail against restraints of all kinds, and fight like a tiger to get your own way. You thrive on competition and actually do your best work in a highly stressful, competitive atmosphere. You love sports and games—anything that provides an outlet for your competitive spirit. If you don't come out on top in any endeavor, you'll try again and again, obsessively, until you either succeed or do yourself harm.

Sometimes it's hard for you to see that your way may not really be the best way, and that alterations are called for. You seek control in every aspect of your life, and making compromises or delegating responsibility is a genuine challenge for you. Therefore, like the leaders of Ancient Rome, you have a tendency to spread yourself too thin and take on more duties than you can realistically handle. You not only take on the higher risks, you embrace them, for they offer the means for you to exert the most control. Like other high rollers, it's often difficult for you to delegate tasks to others, since you view that as a lack of control. Entrepreneurs like you can achieve huge success and overcome the greatest obstacles, but they can also be undone by their own egos and their insatiable will to win. And when they fall, they fall hard. Your motto is, "Don't worry, I have everything under control."

c) More True than False—Low to Moderate Risk

You tend to be fatalistic, but you don't let your fatalism prevent you from seeking success. Unlike your counterpart (a), you are willing to make a substantial effort to achieve success, and you are far more likely to challenge resistance than the true fatalist. Problems surface, however, when you meet greater resistance or more limitations than you deem to be realistic or surmountable. You have a predetermined view of what you can achieve and what you cannot. In other words, your own self-doubts are the largest stumbling blocks preventing you from taking control and achieving major success. Your motto is, "If the peak is too steep, stay on the plateau."

d) More False than True—Moderate to High Risk

This is perhaps one of the best places to be as an entrepreneur when it comes to assessing the odds against you and taking arms against them. While you don't blame Fate for your failures, you are realistic enough to be aware of when you are headed for trouble, and are resilient enough to understand that you must make changes in your approach. You are a determined, take-charge kind of person, but you don't let your struggle for control consume you. You have found a way to take the bitter with the sweet, and can often use the former to your advantage.

You are able to delegate authority while still maintaining a general sense of control over your project. You have a practical, intelligent approach toward competition. When you meet with resistance, you take a step back and observe it in order to overcome it, not unlike a military general meeting resistance from the enemy and falling back to regroup and counterattack. Best of all, you understand yourself and other people, and are willing to make adjustments and compromises to accommodate the needs of consumers, investors, suppliers or industrial clients. In a way, this ability to accept limitations and make compromises is a way to exert your own control, and you know it. With an attitude like this, you will go far. (b), Mr. Top Competitor, may go farther than you, but if he falls, by the time he gets back on his feet, you'll be miles ahead of him. Your motto is, "This is the day the Lord has made. Rejoice and be glad in it and do something with it."

Statement Five:

I am more frightened by the fear of losing than I am excited by the thrill of winning.

a) True—High Risk

While every successful entrepreneur has a healthy respect for failure and an innate desire to avoid it, I think it's safe to say that those who are too afraid

> Fear is rarely helpful for an entrepreneur.

to risk failure will never achieve a major or moderate success while in business for themselves. However, they may become competent company executives and perhaps even earn a substantial salary. A poor decision may or may not cost them their job, and their job is the most that they are willing to risk.

Sure, being an entrepreneur is inherently scary, if you pause to think about it. You intentionally put your livelihood and reputation on the line every time you wake up in the morning and start making business decisions. Some people are naturally timid and cannot get past this initial hurdle. They are like the acrobat who looks down from the high wire and imagines plunging to his death. Either he will fall or go back. The experienced tight wire walker knows the risks, but also knows better than to stare the abyss in the face. If you want to be an entrepreneur, and you cannot get past your fear of risk and loss, think twice about starting an enterprise on your own. Your motto is, "I'm not going to school anymore because every time I pass the Smith's yard, their dog barks at me."

b) False—Low Risk

The true entrepreneur who hungers for success is driven by the desire to win—the higher the risk, the more thrilling the pursuit. Simply put, the more you risk, the more you stand to win or lose. This is where self-confidence comes in. The high risk-taking entrepreneur knows that he or she is up to the challenge of taking a calculated risk. While aware of the negative possibilities, he or she doesn't linger over them. Instead, he or she makes plans for overcoming them. If this is you, then you stand to either win big or lose big, but chances are you'll concentrate on the former and probably achieve it. If you don't, you have enough competitive spirit to pick yourself up and start over again. You wouldn't be able to live with yourself if you didn't. In a way, you are like Capt. James T. Kirk on the original Star Trek series—intelligent, aware, and rational, but also passionate, inventive, and absolutely fearless when the stakes are high.

> We've all known successful enterprises that have been driven onto the rocks by overly-confident leaders focused on the challenge rather than the results.

Do You Have Leadership Potential?

In some cases, extremely enthusiastic entrepreneurs have been known to prefer the thrill of the risk over financial success and a positive image. This drives them to take huge, unrealistically high risks, almost ensuring failure but also supplying the emotional high they live for. So be careful, high roller. Your motto is, "I live on the edge. That's where I'm happiest."

c) More True than False—Low to Moderate Risk

In all likelihood, you have solid entrepreneurial skills or potential and, when push comes to shove, you will take on a higher level of risk than (a). Your fear of risk doesn't totally incapacitate you, but it does hold you back from achieving your fondest dreams and desires. You are a conservative business person, cautious but not terrified. But by the time you work up the self-confidence to strike, the iron may already be cold.

Your biggest challenge is nurturing your confidence in your ability to deal with the financial and personal problems that all entrepreneurs must face, and either conquer or fail to conquer. Too often you "talk yourself out" of taking a calculated risk that in all probability could be your ticket to success. "I don't have the time to do this," you say, or "I don't have the skills," or "This will take more effort than I'm willing to expend." All this amounts to not reaching for the brass ring for fear of falling off your carousel horse. Somewhere fairly early on in your life you learned to doubt yourself, and this doubt carries through to this day, leaving you only half satisfied with your lot. Your motto is, "Yes, but...."

d) More False than True—Moderate Risk

Again, this is a fairly effective, secure attitude for many entrepreneurs. Your chances of becoming extremely successful are somewhat limited, but you will occasionally accept a high-risk project and give it all you've got. You have an admirable level of self-confidence, but it's not all-consuming, and sometimes a twinge of self-doubt will keep you from committing to a project 100%. Sometimes you linger too long over preparation, or do more research when you should be taking action. You long for the thrill of success and you enjoy it, but it is not your main goal. Financial security is important to you, and you can never let go of this need long enough to reach for the heights. You'll get far, but you always have the feeling that something, some innate fear, is holding you back from being the best you can be. Your motto is, "Very good is good enough."

Managing Your Business

7

Managing Your Business 7

The first statements and your responses to them might seem fairly fundamental. In this chapter, we will analyze answers to more complex questions that reveal a deeper level of your entrepreneurial personality and begin to define your entrepreneurial "style." Remember, there is no right or wrong response. More than anything else, this test is an exercise in self-awareness and information-gathering. So let's begin the next leg of the journey.

Statement Six:

I avoid confrontation whenever possible.

a) True—High Risk

If you are the cautious, "make-nice" kind of person who is uncomfortable with changing the norm or challenging those who say, "We've always done it this way," you'll probably always find yourself wondering why fame and riches elude you. If you decide to go into business for yourself, you will likely choose a project that doesn't

> Confrontation is the entrepreneur's constant companion, and to try to avoid it is not only a mistake, it is a sure way to avoid success.

disrupt social convention in any way. Perhaps you'll operate a small, conventional commercial enterprise whose modest success comes from unvarying conformity and uniformity. There's something to be said for the stability of this type of business, but it does not demonstrate much Entrepreneurial Spirit. In general, the entrepreneur thrives on conflicts and strives to confront the norm, shake things up and pull something truly new and improved out of the ashes. If you can't be an innovator and inventor and a challenger on any level—if you'd do practically anything to avoid conflict and original thinking—then you should question whether or not you truly want to go into business for yourself. Your motto is, "Don't rock the boat."

b) False—Low Risk

You are an inventor, an innovator. You constantly look for new ways to approach stubborn problems or stagnant situations. You don't just accept confrontation, you seek it out and jump on it. If you aren't hammering at the gates of conformity, trying to effect a change with a brilliant, unique idea or product, then you're just not satisfied. You love taking the high risks, because you know that high risks require the highest levels of in-your-face, grab-by-the-lapels confrontation of the norm.

You know that those who can change society—which tends to go with the status quo—are those who tend to succeed the most. Look at George Eastman, the Wright Brothers, Thomas Edison, Don Crock, Dr. Benjamin Spock and CoCo Chanel. Their breakthrough inventions and approaches fundamentally changed the ways we travel, communicate, shop, and even the ways we communicate and raise our children. Dr. Martin Luther King, Jr., not an entrepreneur in the strictest sense, brought about huge social changes in the area of civil rights, not by using force, but by using reason. But these

Managing Your Business

people didn't achieve results by offering people predictable answers or by tearing down norms without offering better replacements. No, they were innovators with the courage and self-confidence of five-star generals. They believed in their projects, despite the mockery and criticism of smaller minds mired in tradition.

Problems arise, however, if you lose sight of your objectives and make conflict and confrontation your goals rather than necessary means to an end. The end, of course, is to meet a genuine need, preferably for a large number of people. Your motto is, "If the reward is large enough, I'll fly in the face of conventional wisdom," or "Concepts? I've got a million of 'em!"

> Change for the sake of change is usually meaningless, and forcing an issue without a strategy or larger goal behind the force is wasted effort.

c) More True than False—Low Risk

You may be a conventional thinker, but you're not entirely opposed to questioning the norm. You're much too practical to reject the concept of improving or perfecting something, even when to do so generates a certain amount of uncomfortable conflict. The question is, how much conflict, discomfort, and opposition will you take?

Have you noticed the "clone phenomenon"? Following the introduction of a truly original product that fills a genuine need, markets are flooded with "product clones" that imitate the original but don't improve upon it. Take at-home dry-cleaning products, for instance. The developer behind the original product did most of the development work and assumed most of the risk, breaking ground for competitors and imitators who were only too happy to leap onto the gravy train. Producers of such products are apparently unwilling to risk the criticism that automatically attends the introduction of any product or service that challenges the status quo.

On the other hand, you may be an implementer, a path that many great entrepreneurs have followed. An implementer starts with someone else's original product, service or concept, and modifies it in small but crucial ways in order to take it to distant heights. Dave Thomas, the creator of Wendy's fast food restaurants, was perhaps the best example of this type of businessman. Although Thomas did not originate the concept of fast food, he put his own unique twists on the concept in order to appeal to and secure his own market niches. Your motto is, "Run it up the flagpole and let's see if I can use it."

d) More False than True—Moderate to High Risk

Somewhat more conservative and careful than (c) above, you stand to do well in the long run if you have the persistence to ride out the normal fluctuations of business. You may take on a high-risk project, but, unlike (c), you are probably not going to implement it on a wide basis. Instead, you will attempt to minimize any conflicts connected with it.

Imagine that you are entered in a car race, and neither you nor your fiercest competitors have driven a race car before. Given the choice of a Formula One race car or a BMW high-performance sedan, you choose the latter. Sure, the race car will go faster, but if you don't know how to drive it, you could easily crash. The BMW will get you where you want to go ahead of many of your rivals. But if (b) or (c) figures out how to race his or her temperamental automotive thoroughbred—or build an even faster car—he or she will blaze past you as if you

Managing Your Business

were stationary. This difference of degree in risk-taking is the fundamental difference between you and the more aggressive, innovative types of entrepreneurs. Your motto is, "Clear the mines, then take the field."

Statement Seven:

I find small details bothersome and refuse to deal with them.

a) True—High Risk

Making sure that each "i "is dotted and each "t" is crossed is, in fact, a way to control, avoid or reduce risk. Of course, the lack of a horseshoe nail has destroyed kingdoms before, so it is important to see that those "bothersome details" are, in fact, highly important and must be met. But it is not likely that the high roller will be the one meeting the details. It's not by accident that I have used the word "refuse" in this statement. Many entrepreneurs are a little frightened of making a mistake when they are forced to deal with details, or what they see as "minor matters."

> Generally speaking, the higher the risk a person is willing to take, the less attention he or she will pay to details.

Take this true story, for example. Frank Lloyd Wright, the famous architect, built his most well-known and probably most beautiful residential building, "Fallingwater," so that a large section of the house was cantilevered directly over Bear Run, a swift, cascading stream. The fact that Fallingwater has not become Falling Into Water is an engineering marvel. However, it turns out that Wright had little to do with that miracle. His original plans for the beams supporting the cantilevered section would have sent the magnificent house crashing into the stream in a few years. (To Wright, an insufferable egoist, the length and strength of the beams were trifling details. The beams would have to do what he wanted them to do.) Wright's chief engineer, spotting the flaw in the plans but realizing that Wright would never admit a mistake or change his design, simply went ahead on his own and secretly reinforced the beams. Fallingwater, almost 70 years later, is still an architect's dream but an engineer's nightmare, requiring almost constant maintenance. Recently, every single supporting beam had to be replaced in the cantilevered section.

In this case, attention to detail was needed but ignored by the entrepreneur. Fortunately, he had hired someone who not only knew his job and could be trusted to do it well, but knew enough not to annoy Wright with "technical details." As Walter Gropius, another architect, once observed, "The devil is in the details." The engineer was willing to face the devil, but the artist was not.

The most driven, most dedicated, most passionate entrepreneurs—the high rollers—tend to see the big picture, from start to finish, and little else. They know where to begin, where to go, and how to establish goals, but they have difficulty filling in the details inbetween. This can be a huge benefit, in that they are able to create a strong, guiding vision for their company. They are also adept at identifying essentials and are quick to react to conditions in the marketplace. But if they don't have a trusted ally sweeping up behind them, making sure that small but crucial details are taken care of and that "the numbers add up," they can crash and sink as quickly and easily as the Titanic. If this sounds like you, your motto is, "Attention to details is the hobgoblin of small minds."

b) False—Low to Moderate Risk, Occasionally High

Generally speaking, the person who loves detail work and likes nothing better than to cozy up with a stack of differential equations or tax forms, is not best suited for

Managing Your Business

the entrepreneurial life. They don't want to do the bookkeeping or accounting, the legal work, the office furnishing and supply work, and so on. It's not that they think such work is unnecessary or beneath

> Successful entrepreneurs usually just don't have the time or inclination to handle details that are not an intrinsic part of their visions.

them. They just want someone else to do it so they don't become bogged down in the small picture.

Too often, a love of details results in an inability to make the sweeping, long-range plans that so many projects require. By focusing on the microcosm, one tends to lose sight of the broad vision that drives a company forward and inspires success. The danger of being a detail person is to become swamped by minor considerations, facts and decisions, and, thus, never take a big risk, or see the need to do so. If you cannot raise your head from your needlework, you won't be able to see the wonderful possibilities that await you down the road.

That having been said, details are important, as noted earlier. If your enterprise gets into trouble, knowing the details will sometimes help you locate the source of that trouble. For instance, if you know the entire chain of suppliers that provides materials for your business,

> As you move forward in a business, you'll learn the details of that business, even if it is one you have acquired.

you'll have a very clear understanding of how and why delays develop and what to do to minimize them.

Furthermore, there are some very successful, very talented entrepreneurs who are also natural detail lovers. (If you don't believe this, just read any of Martha Stewart's home decorating books.) While these entrepreneurs enjoy detail work, they are also willing to

123

assume substantial risks to make their projects succeed. For example, before her cookie business went nationwide, the real Mrs. Field took part in and oversaw just about every aspect of her business, including the purchase of ingredients, the selection of cookies to be baked, and the design of the packaging. It was not that she was unable to delegate these responsibilities, for she later did so. She just liked to have a hand in the details.

So if you're a detail person, take heart. It is possible to balance detail work and long-range planning. It just takes more of your precious time and ability. In most cases, as your business grows, you will have to curb your attention to detail in order to manage the wider scope of your enterprise. Your motto is, "The tiniest hole can sink the largest ship."

c) More True than False—Moderate to High Risk

You still find details bothersome, but chances are you won't refuse to handle them yourself. You'll do whatever it takes to make your business succeed, and if that means you'll have to stay up all night calculating figures, so be it. You just won't like it. [Our friend (a) probably wouldn't be capable of doing this.] You can't wait to delegate the detail work to a trusted employee, so you can get back to the planning, researching, networking and pioneering that you love so much and do so well. You'll go far, because you're a big-picture person who has seen first-hand the importance of details. Your motto is, "Get all your ducks in a row, the big ones and the little ones."

d) More False than True—Low to Moderate Risk

You enjoy the detail work, whether you're running your own business or helping someone else run theirs. You also understand that immersing yourself in the details of your business will prevent you from running it effectively. Nevertheless, you gravitate toward writing

Managing Your Business

memos, overseeing product production, and taking care of "little business" whenever you can. That's *you* buying and wrapping Christmas presents for your independent consultants. You won't trust this job to an intern, not even one of your employees. You're not comfortable plotting the course of the company or trying to map its future, but you know you must try. Your biggest challenge is to stop counting the trees, take a big step back, realize that the forest exists and plot a way through it. Delegate most of the detail work to people you trust, and concentrate on growing your enterprise. Your motto is, "There is a universe in a grain of sand."

Statement Eight:

When I make a mistake, I can easily forgive myself and move on.

a) True—High Risk

Self-forgiveness. For most of us, this isn't easy, but there is a select group of men and women who do not let their blunders slow their progress or undermine their determination and self-confidence. These are the high-risk entrepreneurs, the business people willing to put themselves and their projects in jeopardy for the sake of possible high returns. In this rarefied atmosphere, a mistake doesn't count unless it's a deal-breaker.

The (a) person's self-esteem is so high, so impenetrable that his or her mistakes roll right off him or her like water off a soccer ball. Of course, he or she sees the importance of correcting a mistake, and chances are he or she will never make the same one twice. But he or she wastes no time in berating himself or herself or analyzing why he or she fumbled the ball. He or she has the admirable ability to stand up, brush himself or herself off, and get back in the game. His or her

Entrepreneurship Made E-Z

progressive thinking and generosity of spirit usually also extend to his or her staff. Unless an employee makes a disastrous mistake, the high-roller is much more concerned with moving forward and getting past an error than he or she is in assessing blame.

If this describes you, then you are probably a very upbeat, very resilient, assertive, competitive, perhaps even aggressive businessperson. Your eyes are fixed on the prize, and whatever obstacles you encounter on the way

> Everyone makes mistakes, you think, even yourself. The trick is getting past the mistake and learning from it, so that it doesn't happen again.

don't really disturb you unless they seriously impede your progress. Your motto is, "Never look back in anger."

b) False—Low Risk

If you are the type of person who has trouble absolving yourself for every misstep, major and minor, then you will find yourself critically challenged, if not handicapped, in the business world. Why? If you cannot put a mistake behind you, it will haunt you forever, coloring every move you make and inhibiting your desire to take action and move forward. If you have difficulty recovering from a mistake and forgiving yourself for it, you will begin to question every decision you make, or want to make. That original error, and your fixation on it, may damage or even destroy whatever strides you have made. In turn, you will become less sure of your decisions, and hence less willing to take anything but the very lowest risks.

> Striving for excellence is a valid and noble goal, but only as long as you don't let it endanger your business. So don't be so hard on yourself.

Managing Your Business

Your difficulty in granting self-forgiveness could stem from an unrealistic need for perfection, or a deeply-seated need to avoid failure. As the old saying goes, however, "Failure is an excellent teacher." Your motto is, "I'll never forgive myself."

c) More True than False—Moderate to High Risk

Normally you aren't troubled by mistakes, whether they are yours or others. You are more concerned with minimizing or negating the effects of the mistake. But perhaps there are one or two mistakes you've made that you can't seem to forgive yourself for—mistakes that had terrible consequences that you could not undo. It may be very difficult for you to let this kind of mistake go and get on with your business. However, you must, and eventually you will, for you are a self-confident person who believes in the validity of your own ideas and actions.

To help yourself move beyond that persistent mistake from your past, try to find ways to compensate for it. If your unwise decision resulted in the firing of a talented young person, give a chance to someone fresh out of college. Hire him or her and encourage him or her. Or establish a college scholarship. Did your mistake cause a setback in business? Learn from it so that you don't repeat it.

In some cases, a mistake can be turned around to your advantage. For instance, I knew a woman named Ann who ran a gift shop. When she and her head buyer parted company after a fierce argument, Ann decided to specialize in small furnishings and accessories for the home, a move she had always wanted to make but couldn't because her buyer had no expertise in that area. The argument, a silly but sad mistake, was the catalyst for an improvement in Ann's business.

Eventually you will move past all your mistakes, for you know that without your own forgiveness, you will not be able to take the most rewarding risks and achieve your highest level of business potential. Your motto is, "Kiss the past good-bye, and turn toward tomorrow."

d) More False than True—Low to Moderate Risk

Unlike (b), you don't carry your past mistakes around with you like some form of constant penance, but you do have a hard time letting them go. Even little mistakes that don't trouble most business people bother you until you can move past them, and sometimes that takes far too long. By the time you're ready to move on, the competition is a mile down the road and you are eating their dust.

> Making mistakes and correcting them is one way to learn your business.

Forgiving yourself when you make a mistake is a good way to prepare yourself for the inevitable failures and setbacks that occur in any business. This may be a difficult lesson for you, since your self-esteem is not all that strong. However, you are determined and persistent, and these traits alone are a big help in getting past your problems. Your motto is, "I'm working my way back to myself."

Statement Nine:

I do not take myself so seriously that I lose my ability to laugh at myself.

a) True—Moderate to High Risk

People who strive hard for success in business, as well as those who attain it, are subject to the single most debilitating problem that can happen to anyone who wants to improve—a huge ego. A healthy ego is one

Managing Your Business

thing. It's important to have self-confidence and a feeling that you can accomplish whatever you set out to do. It's another thing, though, to feel that you are superior to others because of your business skills, or that you deserve special treatment or unfair advantages.

Remember Frank Lloyd Wright, the megalomaniac architect, and his famous house, Fallingwater? Here was a man who put himself and his creations at the center of everyone's universe. One of the residents of Fallingwater once complained to Wright that water was coming into the dining room and actually falling on his head as he ate dinner. "What should I do?" he asked the architect. Wright's reply: "Move your chair."

Fortunately, *you*, (a), have avoided becoming an insufferable egoist. This is where your good sense of humor comes in. Realizing that we are all human and all have our own failings as well as strong points helps prevent you from developing an ego so large and powerful that it ultimately consumes you. You are one of the fortunate ones whose ego is under control. You can still laugh at yourself. By doing so, you'll find that others will be laughing with you, too, not at you, or worse yet, whispering behind your back.

Remember the late David Thomas, founder of Wendy's Restaurants? We've used him as an example before, mainly because he was truly a gifted businessman. His accomplishments are even more astounding in light of the fact that he did not earn a high school diploma until just a few years before his death in 2002. During his first attempts at cutting a TV commercial, Thomas experienced a lot of difficulty reading the complex scripts written for him. Instead of throwing a tantrum or blaming the writers or refusing to continue—behavior that is all too frequent among celebrities—Thomas laughed at his own mistakes, putting everyone around him at ease. Eventually he suggested that he ad lib the commercials, since he was a highly experienced motivational speaker. The rest is history, and Thomas' round, smiling visage went on to become a familiar image in American households.

Like Dave Thomas, you know that there is only one member of your company that you should be quick to laugh at, and that is yourself. Of course, you don't want to become a laughing stock, but admitting your mistakes, not blaming others and promoting a generally upbeat, friendly atmosphere among your staff will take you far.

Why does someone like you tend to take the sky-high risks? Because you have the self-confidence it takes to believe in yourself and not let minor problems or errors or personal quirks ruffle your feathers. You set your sights high because you know how to use your good humor as a tool to achieve your dreams. Your motto is, "The day I stop laughing at my own mistakes is the day I stop making mistakes."

b) False—Low to Moderate to High Risk

This is one of the few answers that spans the entire range of risk-taking. You're a serious person, and you take yourself seriously, on and off the job. But how successful are you when it comes to actually making and following up on a high-risk decision?

Sometimes children seem to be born serious. If they avoid the company of children and adolescents as they grow up, their

> People are unduly serious about themselves for many reasons.

somber attitude becomes even more entrenched. On the other hand, excessive seriousness could stem from a

Managing Your Business

stern upbringing, serious illness or injury in the past or present, the loss of a loved one, divorce or some other stressful event.

Some relatively successful entrepreneurs are so focused on a technical or specialized skill that they have perfected serious thinking to an art form. These are usually extremely intelligent, dedicated and self-confident people who have one highly-developed talent, skill or concept. Scientists and researchers in general often fall into this category. Clare Patterson, the physicist who calculated the age of the earth, was such a person. So was Charles Tompkins, one of the pioneers of computer science. Although often connected to a university or industry, these people can break away and form their own businesses, and many are very successful entrepreneurs. Some, however, are under so much stress that they succumb to alcoholism, drug use, or even self-delusion.

A person with low self-image can't afford to make fun of himself, lest he appear even weaker than he thinks he is. People lacking in self-confidence generally avoid taking a high or moderate risk, fearing failure and further "proof" of their inferiority. They are usually very self-conscious and hesitant to try out new ideas. Are you in this group? If so, you may be best suited for a low-to-moderate risk business that you can handle on your own, such as a shop or boutique, or a highly specialized service, such as technical writing or photography or a medical specialty. As you gradually become more familiar with success, your self-confidence may rise, allowing you to take greater risks and learn to take yourself less seriously.

> An overtly serious attitude toward oneself, accompanied by an inability to laugh at oneself, is a sign of low self-esteem.

One way to do this is to praise, encourage, and serve others. It seems contradictory, but in doing so you will actually be building a stronger sense of self. Your motto is, "Only a fool laughs at himself."

c) More True than False—Moderate to High Risk

If this is your answer, you are probably an experienced individual with a well-rounded background and a good self-image. As such, you stand poised to become a highly successful entrepreneur. You are an even-tempered person who has achieved a good sense of balance between humor and seriousness, and your self-esteem is not so high that you are egotistical about your abilities or success. Your motto is, "I never met anyone I didn't like, including myself."

d) More False than True—Low to Moderate Risk

You'll laugh at yourself, but not consistently, and not in all cases. Underneath your gentle but determined demeanor, you are somewhat unsure of yourself, a little too self-conscious of how you look and act. You are more social than (b); even so, you feel insecure as a manager. You don't think of yourself as a passionate person, and this may be because you are careful to keep your passion under wraps. A secure atmosphere and a slow, steady rate of progress are your ideals. Your motto is, "Let's all play nice and get along."

Statement Ten:

I am able to work long hours alone when required to do so.

a) True—High Risk

In a way, this is a trick statement. If this is your answer, then you probably feel that you are *always* required to

Managing Your Business

burn the midnight oil at work, as well as the weekend and holidays. Your employees think that your outstanding trait is your dedication to your work. You're also generous, passionate and intelligent, but others will always see you as a workaholic first and anything else second. You're the kind of person whose spouse jokingly asks you, "Have we met before?" You're personable, but you aren't demanding when it comes to the support and encouragement of your associates. You like the company of others, but it's not a necessity. You love your family and friends, but you are so focused on succeeding in your business that it takes precedence over everything else in your life. Your business is your top priority, and you have never hidden this fact. Retirement will be hard on you unless you find an activity to pursue as ferociously as you have pursued your business. In any case, you'll have a hard time handing the reins over to anyone else.

You actively seek the big risks and big payoffs because you *know* you can work hard enough and well enough to achieve the highest level of success. With self-confidence like this, you will succeed in business. Your personal life, however, is another matter entirely. In the best of all worlds, you have found a partner who is able to accept you as you are and not insist on "putting family first." If that's not the case, you may never have a truly satisfying home life. Your motto is, "Nothing truly worthwhile ever got accomplished by itself."

> Hard work and dedication alone won't make a successful entrepreneur, but they are critical elements to your success.

b) False—Low Risk

You're a Taurus, aren't you? I say this half in jest, because people born under the astrological sign of Taurus the Bull are supposed to be the most dedicated family men and women in the universe. You're a hard worker, but you're not working hard to become a highly successful businessperson, improve the lives of millions of people, or make your mark as a captain of industry. You're working hard to support your family, or to satisfy your parents or in-laws or close friends. And that's a big difference. You truly worship your spouse and adore your children, and family always comes first—not product development or marketing. While you are creative and have excellent powers of concentration, you hate being alone and are at your happiest when surrounded by friends and family. Football games, class reunions, Thanksgiving dinner at Grandma's, and vacations at Universal Studios are your ideas of paradise.

You may have your own business—a garage, a store, or a professional practice—but you also have a schedule, and you try very hard to stick to it. Holidays are important to you, and you have yet to miss a single Christmas (or Chanukah or Kwanza) with the family. No one can knock your lifestyle—and you are probably a consummately happy person. But you are not a very successful entrepreneur. Your motto is, "I've never seen a headstone that read, 'I should have spent more time at work.'"

c) More True than False—Moderate to High Risk

This situation represents a kind of middle ground between the "my-business-is-my-life" entrepreneur and the family-friendly Taurus. No, you'll never be a true high-roller, unless you stay single, because you won't risk your family's security. That's one high risk you'll never take. On the other hand, you don't hesitate to work long hours alone, up to a point, and you have the only kids on the block who know their dad's/mom's office better than their own bedrooms. Your greatest moments of self-conflict will revolve around spending time at work versus spending time with your family and friends.

Managing Your Business

Which choice you ultimately make will depend upon your upbringing, religion, age, and other factors. Your motto is, "I'm the only person I know who has a collection of paper dolls cut out of blueprint paper."

d) More False than True—Low Risk

Go ahead, spend more time with your spouse and kids. You might as well, because your level of risk-taking is about the same as Mr. and Ms. Taurus. Like them, you feel uncomfortable when you are alone, working late into the night. Oh, you'll do it if you feel you must, and you won't complain about it loudly, like the Taurus, but your heart will not be in the work. Like a Taurus, a small, conventional business of your own, able to meet your family's needs, is just about perfect for you. Your motto is, "East, West, home's best."

Risks, Goals, and Change

8

Risks, Goals, and Change

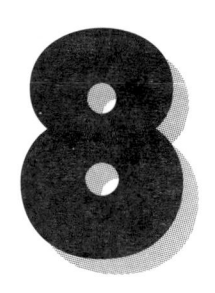

In this chapter, we continue exploring your test results, but now the statements become more focused and responses get more complex and more involved as we deal with the most challenging issues that confront the new entrepreneur. How you view your contributions to society, how you deal with change, and how you structure your life in order to maintain and grow your business are all addressed here. What kind of entrepreneur are you? You are well on your way to finding out!

Statement Eleven:

I believe that I have something valuable to contribute to society.

a) True—High Risk

That makes sense, doesn't it? The person who is 100% convinced that he or she can make the world a safer, healthier, more convenient, or more amusing place is someone who is willing to risk a lot to turn that belief into a reality. Look at Walt Disney, for example. Here was a man with a difficult childhood who was determined to make other kids' childhoods happier. During the early days of the Disney studio, Mickey Mouse's creator constantly skated on the brink of bankruptcy. At one point, he and his wife were living in a house that resembled a shed. He even lost the rights to his first successful cartoon character to his financial backer. But nothing stopped Disney from fulfilling his belief in making magic for children and the young at heart. And as everyone knows, he went on to establish one of the most profitable, most innovative, most creative businesses of all time.

Inventors and innovators know they can make a large, positive impact on society, and they are hellbent on doing it.

> Inventors and innovators frequently have a deep, abiding belief in the value of their projects.

Thomas Edison, Alexander Graham Bell, Marie Curie, Louis Pasteur all knew that their work would be of massive benefit to society. Not all of these great people benefited from their discoveries, but most of them did, and in a big way, too. Theirs is a special kind of dedication that springs, not just from the desire to make a handsome profit, but from nobler aspirations.

Do you have such noble goals? Would you like to combine benefiting humanity with making yourself a lot of money? Based upon what you want to achieve, however, you may have a long, risky, challenging journey ahead of you, since people are usually resistant to change. If you have the courage of your convictions, you will prevail. However, if your desire to become well-known for your contribution takes over your quest, you could develop a monumental ego, and that almost always signals trouble, if not the beginning of a decline. So ask yourself, "Can I handle fame and fortune and maintain a healthy ego?" Your motto is, "I will make the world a better place."

Risks, Goals, and Change

b) False—Low to Moderate Risk

Let's reveal your motto first, because it says it all: "Go with the flow."

"Sure," you say, "I'd like to benefit society." But providing a wide variety of athletic footwear in your shoe store seems like a good way to go about it. By aiming low in the aspiration department, you know you'll hit your target every time. Now, on the other hand, you may be a hard worker when it comes to donating your time at the local soup kitchen, or helping recent immigrants learn to read English. So you may have an impact on society. It just won't be through your business. You're a conventional business owner or intrapreneur, and you enjoy your creature comforts. You're just not willing to stake whatever business assets you have acquired for the possibility of benefiting others. Is this self-centered? Or is it just practical?

Perhaps you simply do not have an earth-shattering discovery or breakthrough service or invention that is going to end up in the history books, nor do you have any interest in backing someone who does. What you do have is the ability to maintain the status quo. You keep on plugging away. You understand the importance of having a viable market, but you are mostly in business for personal gain, and you are satisfied with fairly low-risk yields. Another motto for you might be, "If it ain't broke, don't fix it. And if it is broke, see if you can still use it."

c) More True than False—Moderate to High Risk

You are a driven person, committed to your idea or project, and determined to help society. Perhaps someone did you a favor once, or saved you from certain failure, and you want to give back a little of what you have received. Or perhaps you are a people lover, a socialist in the best sense of the word, and you long to improve the lot of humankind. You've discovered a need that isn't being filled, and you know you can meet it. You are not as passionate about your mission as (a), but you are quietly resolute. You're willing to take some pretty high risks in order to make your dreams come true, but you don't eat, sleep, and breathe your project to the extreme extent that (a) does. You would be torn if you had to risk your family's welfare on your perceived "contribution to society." Somehow you just can't bring yourself to take that extra step into near-fanaticism that comes all too easily for (a). Your practical nature holds you back. Your motto is, "I'd like to make the world a better place."

d) More False than True—Low to Moderate Risk

You might feel that you have something to contribute to society and the world at large, but you frequently question yourself, your project, your commitment, and your own self-confidence.

If you, (a), (b) and (c) have agreed to make a bungee jump for charity, (a) and (c) will cheerfully leap off the platform, (b) will recant, and you will waffle. You'll retie your shoes, check out the crowds, speculate on the weather—anything to postpone making the jump. In the end, chances are almost even that you will jump. But you might have to be pushed.

Face it. You are more focused on making a profit, here and now. Society will go on without your help, and someone else will meet those large, juicy, genuine needs while you clean up the smaller ones that really won't make much impact. You don't need to create an empire or earn the abiding love of humanity, though those would be nice. You aim lower, but your hit ratio is greater. You lack the necessary level of self-confidence required to tackle the big risk, or the towering challenge.

Risks, Goals, and Change

Your motto is, "I'd rather contribute to myself than anyone else."

Statement Twelve:

I welcome change.

a) True—High Risk

Heroditus, the famous ancient Greek historian, once claimed, "The only thing certain is change." Not only do you agree with him, you take his statement a step further and say, "I'm really glad that the only thing certain is change." You thrive on change and the challenges it brings, and you welcome competition for the same reason. On the other hand, the prospect of stagnation and stasis scares you to death.

Why should anyone want change, especially if he or she is enjoying success? Well, perhaps you believe that, no matter how well you are succeeding, you can always do better, and the only way you are likely to do so is to ride the waves of change. You may falter for a while, even sink beneath the surface. But that only makes your triumphant surge to the top that much more dramatic and enjoyable. You are also practical enough to realize that change will happen, whether you want it to or not. You might as well be prepared for it and take advantage of it.

The entrepreneur who loves to take a high risk will not only welcome change but seek it, even try to predict it. If you are this kind of entrepreneur, you are constantly reading and researching, getting a feel for the pulse of the economy and looking for targets of opportunity. Of course, this really means that you are trying to forecast "the next big thing" so you can benefit by being the first one at the table when change shows up.

Let's take a look at one of my favorite entrepreneurs, George Eastman, who was born in 1854. George became interested in photography at the age of 23, when planning for a trip abroad. He wanted to take a camera with him, but was discouraged because of the size, bulk, and expense of the equipment and the difficulty in operating it.

After this disheartening experience, George became obsessed with the idea of developing a small, portable, affordable camera for the common man. After three years of experimenting with homemade gelatin emulsions in his mother's kitchen, George invented and patented the dry plate that would become the basis for modern cameras. As he was to write years later: "The idea gradually dawned on me that what we were doing was not merely making dry plates, but that we were starting out to make photography an everyday affair…to make the camera as convenient as the pencil."

George and his partner, Henry Strong, faced serious challenges as they set about changing the face of photography. Once, they had to replace an entire batch of dry plates that had gone bad. "Making good on those plates took our last dollar," George once said, "but what we had left was more important—reputation."

In 1888, George released the first Kodak camera (a name that he coined). It cost $25 and had 100 exposures. New film could be inserted for a $10 charge. Thanks to George's innovative technology, the company grew quickly, but its long-term sustained growth depended upon George's foresight. He insisted on continued research and development to prevent the company from losing its competitive edge. In addition, he hired highly competent employees, whom he paid well, consistently poured his profits back into the company, and expanded into other markets.

Risks, Goals, and Change

Did George take a gigantic risk? Absolutely, but a calculated one. It was always possible that people would not be willing, confident or patient enough to take their own pictures. But George counted on Americans' spirit of independence and their love of convenience and thrift to help him change the world. And they did.

> Being able to use the power of change in your favor, and even create change, is a powerful asset.

Like George Eastman, you don't just withstand the tornado. You try to foresee its path, then harness its force to help yourself and others. You are a rare spirit, and if you win, you will win very big.

One company that was almost destroyed by change managed to make change work in its favor. The company was Church & Dwight, owners of the Arm & Hammer label and makers of baking soda, used primarily in baking. In the 1970s, as women began entering the workforce in droves, fewer and fewer people continued to bake from scratch. They just didn't have the time. Baking soda sales plummeted. After some intelligent research, Arm & Hammer discovered that many of the people still buying their product were not using it for baking at all. Since the soda was excellent at absorbing odors, people were using it as a deodorant in refrigerators and bathrooms. Responding to the market's changing needs, the company did a 180-degree turnaround and began developing an entire product line of deodorants and healthcare items, including toothpaste and foot powder. Not only was Arm & Hammer flexible

> The winds of change will crush most entrepreneurs. Others will bend with the winds, and change slowly. But you will ride the winds and use them to shape the future.

145

enough to turn change into success, they were smart enough to listen to their customers who found their own creative uses for a seemingly staple product.

Do you embrace change? Do you seek it out? Do you see it as an opportunity rather than a limitation? Are you never satisfied to rest on your laurels, no matter how much you have accomplished? Do you practically beg your competitors to challenge you by improving upon your products? Day by day, are you determined to rise to the challenge of a changing world and meet its needs head on? If so, then you have what it takes to become the next George Eastman, Dave Thomas, D.W. Griffith or Bill Gates and ride the winds of change to the top of the mountain. Your motto is, "A shift in the weather is coming. I know just how to adjust my sails."

b) False—Low Risk

If you had your way, you'd live and work in a perfectly static world. You'd continue to make your product, and people would continue to buy it. It would never improve or degrade, and people's needs would never vary. You cherish routine and permanence. Unfortunately for you, the modern world is not static, and no one can live in a vacuum, at least for very long. It is extremely difficult if not impossible for you to raise your head above your cozy existence to glimpse the swirling future as it bears down upon you, threatening to change your life and that of everyone else by knocking you upside down.

You long to go back in time, to a simpler way of life, when change came more slowly and gently than it does today. The technological revolution signaled by the popularity of computers plunged you into shock. You're still recovering from the Industrial Revolution. While you're not making buggy whips, you concentrate on a basic product or service that fills a large, basic need, or a

Risks, Goals, and Change

small, specialty need. If you provide the former, you're swamped with competition, and it is difficult for you to carve a profitable niche in your market. If it's the latter, then you are challenged to create a profitable market base. Still, you view change as your enemy rather than a wonderful opportunity, so you brace yourself to withstand change, rather than rushing to embrace it. But this can be disastrous.

Remember the Rolodex? This was a small, rotating mechanical device used to hold address cards in alphabetical order. Designed to take up little space on a desk, the Rolodex allowed the business executive or office clerk to find addresses and phone numbers quickly and easily. In its time (the 1950s to the mid 1980s), the Rolodex was an absolute essential for every office worker. Today, you'd be hard pressed to find a handful of these little dinosaurs in use, since even tiny hobby stores and secondhand bookstores are online.

It is a force that moves through time, like the weather. If you don't welcome it and use it, you have two choices: withstand it or be destroyed by it. Because you know in your heart that your position is precarious, you can't force yourself to take the bigger risks associated with those who learn from changes. Your motto is, "Remember the good old days?"

> Change is not a matter of chance.

c) More True than False—Moderate to High Risk

Like (a), you too welcome change. However, you are less likely to go out looking for it than the high-roller. You're not proactive when it comes to change. You are intelligently reactive. Fortunately for you, you are all too aware of the inevitability and power of change, and when it's brought to your attention that the marketplace is changing, you go into "storm watch" mode. You are quick to take action and prepare for a host of possibilities, fortifying your weak spots and seeking opportunities for growth.

You know better than to respond to every variable and fluctuation that comes down the pike. In the face of significant change, you carefully determine your course by considering all your possibilities. You might decide to stay right where you are and let change descend upon you. Or perhaps you decide to make major or minor alterations in your business to accommodate the change. You also consider how best to make these changes. This is a very practical and profitable approach to weathering and profiting from the constant changes in the business climate. Your motto is, "Change is inevitable. Mediocrity is not."

d) More False than True—Low to Moderate Risk

You do react to change, but you are not fast on your feet. An opportunity may come and go before you decide to act on it. There is an upside and a downside to being a little slow to react to change. On the positive side, you will not be buffeted about by the whims of the marketplace. The more quickly you change, and the more drastic the changes you make, the more you risk undercutting the reputation you have been trying to create ever since you were in business.

For example, imagine that you own an upscale, highly competitive restaurant. If your business is predicated on offering high quality beef dinners at an affordable price, what happens when consumers suddenly begin shunning beef as unhealthy? Do you add other dishes to your menu? Do you shift your emphasis to poultry and seafood? Let's say you try the latter approach. Suddenly there is a salmonella scare and your restaurant looks like

Risks, Goals, and Change

a natural history museum at two in the morning. And there is a mercury poisoning scare right around the corner. Holding fast in the face of change, or at least initiating change slowly, is sometimes the best policy, especially when it is all but impossible to predict what changes you will have to deal with next.

In most cases, though, you are at a decided loss if you are constantly ignoring changes in your business, failing to respond quickly enough, or failing to make the best adjustments. For a positive example, take the career of William Wrigley, of Wrigley's gum fame. He started out in the late 1800s in Philadelphia, hawking his father's scouring soap in the streets. Later, selling the soap from a horse and wagon, he handed out packets of baking powder as customer premiums, and when the baking powder became more popular than the soap, he promptly switched the focus of his company. Still later, when chewing gum premiums topped the popularity of the baking powder, Wrigley was cognizant enough of change to eventually switch products again. The rest is history.

Because you are inclined to hedge your bets and reduce your risk, it is unlikely that you will be able to take advantage of the truly life-transforming changes when they do come along, as Wrigley was able to do. Your motto is, "What do I look like, a chameleon? I'll make changes when I'm good and ready."

> When you make a change, however, you also take a calculated risk.

149

Statement Thirteen:

I can plan for the future and still take care of day-to-day activities.

a) True—High Risk

In all honesty, I really hope that you chose this answer. If you didn't, then you are in for more than a little difficulty in operating your business. You are in general a person who takes high risks, but you know that apportioning your time is one of the few areas where it's a good idea not to take big risks. An over-emphasis on any aspect of your business—the big picture of vision and planning, or the little picture of the routine necessities—could easily result in failure.

Being a successful entrepreneur always means walking a fine line between maintaining and pursuing a grand vision and taking care of those pesky little routine activities that can drive you crazy but will sink your ship, and your vision, if you ignore them. If you chose this answer, you are not only a well-balanced thinker, both practical and creative, you are also a juggler. You constantly hold your brilliant plans for your company's growth in front of your face, and your employees' faces, while juggling more mundane tasks—paying bills, hiring and training

> If your business involves a plant as well as an office, or several branch offices, then your task will be that much more challenging.

employees, finding adequate storage space, keeping books, scheduling and keeping appointments, and so on at the same time. Some of these tasks can be delegated to other people, but a smart businessperson will keep a hand in the day-to-day running of the business and be aware of everything that impacts its operation.

Risks, Goals, and Change

This situation reminds me of a man I once knew named Randall, a bright, energetic fellow with a truly innovative product for the scientific community. Randall produced and marketed a small electronic monitoring device that greatly enhanced the speed and accuracy of counting and identifying very small particles. Because he soon had more orders than he could fill, he was forced to expand, and ended up expanding too rapidly. He became so focused on meeting product orders that he wasn't prepared when his customers began to complain about the quality of his monitors. Apparently, without Randall's approval, one of his suppliers had modified the design of a key component in order to cut costs, and this had lessened the efficiency of the monitor. One of his employees had noticed the change and had brought it to his boss' attention, but Randall, swept up in his latest plans for expansion, ignored the warning. Had he been more involved in the product design and supply sides of his business, Randall would have seen the significance of the alteration immediately and dealt with the problem before it could have a major effect on his business. As it was, he almost lost two of his largest customers, and had to find a new supplier, who charged more for the new product than the original.

Fortunately for Randall, he was able to turn this near-disaster into a valuable lesson in balancing and juggling his business priorities. In the future, he set time aside every month to look into every aspect of his business—looking for potential problems and correcting them before they made an appreciable impact. No part of his business, including office supply stock, was beneath him. If you have achieved this happy balance, then your motto is, "If it wouldn't be for the trees, there wouldn't be a forest." The genius is to see both at the same time.

151

Entrepreneurship Made E-Z

b) False—Low Risk

You've heard of Wolfgang Amadeus Mozart, one of the most famous composers who ever lived, if not the most famous. At one time the darling of Austria's royal court and the toast of the town, Mozart died in his mid-thirties, too impoverished to afford a simple funeral. How did the undisputed king of music in the 18th century—or probably any century—sink to this depth of poverty and despair?

Mozart's music is filled with exquisite complexity, and so was the rest of his life. But the only details he noticed were in his compositions. A too-generous friend, he gave away large sums of money to people he barely knew, and soon unscrupulous people were taking advantage of his naiveté and his giving nature. Extravagant in his own purchases, he failed to keep track of his debts and expenses. In short, his mind was focused exclusively upon the area in which he excelled, and all others were meaningless to him.

On the level of art alone, Mozart succeeded brilliantly, but he was a catastrophe when it came to business or personal finances. Whether you look only at your vision, or only at the balance sheet, you cause a lack of balance that will ultimately cause the fall of your enterprise.

What happens when you concentrate only on the big picture? If this is the case, you might not delegate routine tasks to other people because you cannot even see the tasks. Obviously you're not doing them yourself. Like Mozart, you see only the splendor of your vision, ideas and talents. Practical concerns, such as paying the bills and scheduling customers, have no place in your plans, even if such concerns are not "minor details" but essential aspects of doing business. Routine considerations are the basis of any business, brilliant or

Risks, Goals, and Change

otherwise, and if you do not attend to them and make sure that they are handled promptly and accurately, your project is doomed. You normally don't go after the high risks, but in reality, by failing to plan for both the future and the present, you are taking one of the highest risks in business.

What happens when you concentrate on the daily operation of the enterprise and ignore the future? The business stagnates, and eventually withers and dies, or is obliterated in a merger or consolidation. Taking care of the business of business is not the same as the business itself, and someone with passion, foresight and drive is needed to take any enterprise forward into its next, more profitable phase.

> Without someone to expedite growth and, when necessary, change, any business will at best just manage to survive.

If either of these two scenarios describes you, you are taking a big chance, and the odds of achieving and sustaining success are stacked against you. Just surviving will be a constant struggle. Forget about expansion and increasing profits. It's not a matter of "if" your project will fail, but merely when. The question is, can you amass enough profit to get you started and keep you going in another area before the inevitable happens?

If you feel inundated with routine tasks, maybe you need to hire someone to keep them in line. Just don't forget to keep abreast of every aspect of your business, even if it means touching base with your employees at the start or end of the day. Without some sense of connection to the everyday needs of your business, you will rapidly lose sight of both your

> Day-to-day tasks may seem boring, but paying the bills and taking routine calls are what keeps a business going.

capabilities and your responsibilities, and this will spell danger for your enterprise in general.

If you lack the vision, passion, and determination to see the big picture, you are in even deeper trouble, for you cannot hire an employee to provide inspiration for your business. Your best bet would be to find a dynamic, far-sighted partner, then split the duties accordingly. Your motto is, "What trees?" or "What forest?" [See (a) above.]

c) More True than False—Moderate Risk

You try to balance the big picture with the daily routine, but you are not always effective in doing so. You vacillate one way or the other, for your talents lie in one of these two directions, not in both. Perhaps you are a Seer, full of ideas and concepts and viable ways to execute them all. An excellent communicator, you enchant prospective customers and impress merchants, suppliers, and agents of all kinds. When it comes to bookkeeping or payments, you hesitate, but you will tackle the most stupefying number-crunching if you have to, or at least find a competent person to do it for you. You don't like answering letters or handling complaints or meeting deadlines, but you'll do it if you have to, and you'll do it reasonably well. Or perhaps you are a scribe, loving the work that seems logical to you but much less sure about making plans for the future and getting others to believe in those plans. In other words, when push comes to shove, you can personally handle or at least delegate every aspect of your business.

Most people probably fall into this category, and that is why most people do not work for themselves, or by themselves. No one wants this much responsibility. The stress alone generated by this sort of lifestyle is numbing. Your motto is, "Let's see how long can I balance these eleven bowling balls on my head."

Risks, Goals, and Change

d) More False than True—Moderate Risk

Doing a poor to mediocre job of balancing the future with the present is much less effective than admitting defeat and looking for assistance. If this is your answer, then

> Most business people can afford someone to take on at least some of the clerical activities, but more than one person may be necessary.

you definitely need help, either with planning or routine tasks. Again, a partner may be useful to anyone who has trouble balancing the different kinds of workloads that are part and parcel of any business. Your motto is, "Would someone please take these bowling balls off my head?"

Statement Fourteen:

I am excellent at prioritizing.

a) True—High Risk

The statement above is really an extension of Statement Thirteen regarding future and present needs. If you are balancing your vision of your company with its everyday needs, then you know how to prioritize when it comes to running a business.

Like Statement Thirteen, setting, maintaining and adjusting your priorities is a low-risk activity, even though you are prone to taking higher risks. Taking some high risks is the

> Those who fail to set priorities, or set inappropriate priorities, are the ones who are needlessly risking their company's stability.

sign of a good entrepreneur. Taking foolishly high risks, like failing to make wise priorities, is the sign of a fool.

If you have chosen this answer, then you are dedicated to succeeding in your business and are committed to making it work. While your company will probably always be your top priority, or close to it, you also see the wisdom in being flexible on a day-to-day, week-to-week, month-to-month basis. You have realized that you must be flexible enough to handle problems when or before they arise, on a week-to-week, even a day-to-day basis. You know how to shift priorities as your situation demands it.

Let's say you have made a conscientious effort to grow your budding software business. This means hours of networking and making contacts, meetings, phone calls, planning, and research—hours when you are either out of the office or in virtual isolation. If, during this period, a virus begins wreaking havoc with your staff's computers, you will immediately shift your priorities to handle the emergency, which has struck at the very heart of your business. But what if the situation were less obvious? Perhaps two co-workers are not getting along, and their friction is beginning to have a markedly negative effect on the work climate. If you are truly a real pro at setting and resetting priorities, you will get to the bottom of this conflict before it poisons all your employees and destroys your business. This is in spite of the fact that you would much prefer to sit in your office, ignore the bickering, and make those contacts with your competitor's clients.

How do you know how, where, and when to set or change your priorities? Chances are, if you chose this response, you have an innate feel for the answers to that question. No doubt you have an intuitive sense of when your enterprise is working smoothly and it is safe to try to expand, and when danger threatens in any area of the business. Is it a new, gung-ho competitor? Is it an unexplained slow-down in profits? Is it weak advertising or a lack of effective advertising? Is it a new trend that

Risks, Goals, and Change

you must address, one way or the other? Whatever the threat, you are attuned to your company and your employees, and you have a good feel for all the aspects of your business, big and small, down the road or in the present. You also know when a problem has grown large enough to require immediate solution. You won't let any problem become so large that it threatens the well-being of your company.

As mentioned before, your top priority is creating a profitable enterprise, and expanding it is probably your next priority. In the back of your mind, no matter what else happens, the health and success of your enterprise is your guiding light and, for the meantime, your ultimate goal. But you are open-minded enough to see how day-to-day business, personal interactions and other aspects of running a company impact upon its success, and you will put your long-range priority on hold to address other issues that are, at any given point, more critical.

As an entrepreneur, you have made a secret pact with yourself (whether you know it or not) that your business will, at least for a while, take priority over other aspects of your life. Your personal life, your family and friends, your social contacts, and your interests and hobbies will all take a back seat, and the least important will probably go dormant. It's a sad fact but true: Starting a business requires an enormous commitment in terms of time and effort, and you will have very little time or inclination left to share with anyone else. If you have chosen this answer, you have already made the decision to put your business first. To be frank, many families cannot stand the kind of friction and stress created by this situation, and it is particularly hard for children to bear. Keep this in mind as you make

> Organizing priorities goes beyond business life, of course.

your business Priority One. Your motto is, "Creating and maintaining at least one successful business is my top priority in life."

b) False—Low Risk

Perhaps you have established your priorities, and business is not Priority One. There is nothing wrong with this decision, as long as you are aware that you have made it. Perhaps you choose to spend more time with your family, and devote less time to your business. Perhaps you have trustworthy colleagues or employees who can run the business for you, to some extent, and you are content to continue on that level. Or maybe you have other commitments that take up more of your time, energy and interest than your work does. You're in business for yourself because of the independence you've discovered working for yourself. Financial success is nice but not necessary, as far as you are concerned. We will discuss this type of entrepreneur, whom I call a *car owner*, later in the book.

> Suffice it to say that there are millions of small-business owners who sustain themselves and their families with small ventures, yet derive their real satisfaction from other sources.

But what if you are truly trying to succeed at your own business, yet keep failing to establish the priorities that would help you achieve your goal? This is a problem, and it could prove to be a lethal one for the independent business person. It is, in fact, a very risky way to proceed in business, even though you are adverse to risk. By not setting appropriate priorities, or by failing to consistently follow them, you put the health of your enterprise in grave jeopardy.

Risks, Goals, and Change

People who try to do too much, too quickly, often have this problem. Consider an acquaintance of mine, called Jeffrey, who bought a fairly successful mail-order vitamin business. Instead of focusing on slow, steady growth, Jeffrey became enchanted with the idea of expanding his market by setting up chain stores throughout his state, then his region. When the opportunity came along to expand nationwide, he jumped at the chance, although the mail-order business was already beginning to falter. Under the guidance of his new advertising agency, Jeffrey added a line of homeopathic remedies and weight-control products. When some of his stores began performing badly, Jeffrey tried to resuscitate the catalog business, but his efforts were too little, too late. He was exploring the idea of marketing exotic teas when his business finally collapsed underneath him, landing him in bankruptcy, bitterly complaining about the fickleness of the American consumer.

But Jeffrey's problem was not his customers. It was his inability to set a top priority and focus upon it. Instead, he leaped from product to product, market to market, method to method, virtually abandoning his core business for trendy, risky projects that he promptly abandoned when they began to show signs of weakness.

To achieve soundness of your company, you will have to set some other priorities, including the hiring of competent, trustworthy personnel, conducting careful product and market research, and focusing on collections as well as sales. Without establishing these basic priorities while preserving the flexibility to prevent or resolve problems as they develop, you decrease your chances

> If you are committed to achieving financial success, then the soundness of your company should be your top priority.

159

for business success. However, admitting that you have difficulty in establishing priorities is a good first step toward overcoming your weakness in this area. Enlist the assistance of a trusted partner or associate to help you set priorities and stick to them within reason. Your motto is, "This, that, and the other thing are all equally important."

c) More True than False—Low Risk

You are committed to making your business successful. This is your Number One priority. Where you sometimes run into problems is creating a hierarchy of subsequent priorities. When you go into business for yourself, it is easy to become swamped with details and overwhelmed with the complexities of ordering and operating your venture. A hundred aspects of the business all seem to be crying out for attention, all at the same time. Fortunately, when you feel overwhelmed by competing priorities, you can regroup and refocus upon your top priority. This will always help you reorient yourself and redirect your efforts.

> The key for you is to simplify your priorities, keeping in mind the basic goal of maintaining a sound business.

Your list of priorities will vary, depending upon the size of your company, your market, the type of product or service you offer, and other variables. Here is a "short list" of priorities that worked for me when I was establishing Transmedia, and every single one of my employees could understand and recite this list:

- Get restaurants (to participate in the program)
- Get cardholders (to sign onto the program)
- Keep track of every detail (so that the back office can run efficiently)

Risks, Goals, and Change

If you are dedicated to running a successful company, almost nothing will sink it faster than permanently losing sight of your top priorities. Therefore, if you are having difficulty maintaining priorities or returning to them after settling emergencies, set aside a day every week to concentrate on dealing with each of your key priorities. In time, you can reduce this schedule to one day a month, or assign a trusted associate to help keep you focused upon your top priorities.

I am reminded of a friend named Bud who not only took advantage of an opportunity when it presented itself, but also was able to "roll with the punches" and hold tight to his chief priority, even when his business was threatened. Bud was determined to set up a small grocery delivery business to supply families on military bases. Unable to get sufficient supplies, Bud was ready to retire his delivery van when a banker casually suggested that Bud deliver frozen food. Bud immediately resuscitated his dream, equipping his van, and later several others, with refrigerated lockers. He went on to build a very successful organization, which he sold. Eventually he moved to Florida and established one of the largest food brokerage firms in the United States. Instead of abandoning his concept, he stayed with it and modified it until it brought him, in stages, the success he hoped for. If you are like Bud, your motto is, "I stick to my basic priorities like glue."

d) More False than True—Moderate Risk

You are in essentially the same position as (c) above. Your only difference is one of degree. It is harder for you to establish priorities, and, therefore, it is probably incumbent upon you to proceed more slowly than either (a) or (c), especially in terms of expanding your business. To try to grow your business without having firm

Entrepreneurship Made E-Z

priorities would only produce disaster, as was the case with Jeffrey and his vitamin business.

Fortunately, you are probably not in the position of (b), who must either keep his ambitions very low, or rely upon employees and associates to keep him focused on priorities. Of course, as your company grows and becomes more complex, you may choose to hire people to help ensure that you meet your basic priorities. This will leave you more time to concentrate upon ways to increase business and grow the enterprise.

You must take great care not to let problems or incipient problems distract you from Priority One, even though you must develop the flexibility to identify and resolve problems promptly. Your motto is: "A sound business is Priority One."

> Whatever you do, do not lose sight of your main goal of maintaining a healthy and thriving business. All other priorities must be predicated on this one.

Statement 15—Essay Question

Imagine that you are at a convention geared to your industry.

You are either:

A) a major executive of a large company, hosting a hospitality room for all the owners of various smaller companies with whom you do business

B) the owner of one of these small companies

Which position would you prefer to hold? Why?

A) You have chosen to be a major executive in a large company. In this particular scenario, although you are interacting with owners of smaller companies, i.e.,

Risks, Goals, and Change

entrepreneurs, you are not yourself, strictly speaking, an entrepreneur. You have most, if not all, the responsibilities of an entrepreneur, and you plan and care for your business in the same ways as effective entrepreneurs do. Nevertheless, there is one fundamental difference between you and the other people in that hospitality suite: You do not own your own business.

Therefore, chances are that you are hard-working and dedicated. You're also fairly competitive and creative. Unfortunately, you either need to build your self-confidence and experience, or encounter the right opportunity, before you make the big move and go into business for yourself.

I'd like to introduce a maritime analogy that I believe is very useful for illustrating the difference between entrepreneurs and intrapreneurs, such as business executives. An intrapreneur is an employee, albeit sometimes an extremely important, influential and responsible employee. In this sense, an intrapreneur is like the captain of an old-time tea clipper. In the late 19th century, these beautiful, swift sailing ships were used to convey tons of raw tea leaves from China and India to England to satisfy the British obsession for a "cuppa." Fortunes were made or lost, based upon the speed of the ship and the skill of her captain.

However, in the great majority of cases, the captains of these vessels were not the owners. No matter how skilled they were or devoted to the ship and her sailors, once the voyage was over, the captains had no say in the fate of their ships. The owner could decide to sell the ship or put it under the command of another skipper, or dismantle it or put it into dry dock or even destroy it, and the captain could do nothing to stop the owner's decision. In addition, the captain received a flat fee for his services, plus a bonus if he completed his voyage ahead of schedule. It was the owner(s) of the clipper ship who both decided her fate and benefited most from her successful ventures.

However, the captain was responsible for the ship during her dangerous voyage around the Cape of Good Hope and across the China Sea. It was up to the captain to get the clipper to the Orient and back in one piece, intact, with her precious cargo in good shape and all hands alive and accounted for. If the captain wished, he could get the commission of another, different ship. His future was not tied to a particular vessel. However, many captains went on to become full or partial owners of their own fleets.

You, the intrapreneur, are like the captain of that clipper ship. You make major decisions regarding the welfare and success of the company you work for, but your fate is not necessarily tied to the fate of the company. If you leave Company A to perform similar duties for Company B, Company A will go on without you, experiencing at most only a short period of transition. You may receive some praise for your efforts, but most of the credit for the success of the company, as well as the greatest monetary rewards, will go to the entrepreneur who started the company (or took it over and made it successful). You may enjoy your work and the sense of power you get from performing your crucial duties, but you do not have either pride of ownership or absolute power regarding the fate of the company.

However, being the "captain" isn't such a bad place to be. For one thing, you enjoy a responsible position without having the burden of making final decisions. And, being an intrapreneur is excellent training for learning the entrepreneurial skills you will need if you ever decide to

Risks, Goals, and Change

start your own company. In addition, it is very unlikely that any error you make will result in the downfall of the company. (If your work isn't at least competent, you'll probably never make it to the executive level.)

It is true that you probably won't get to enjoy that hospitality suite very much. Networking with the suppliers is a work assignment for you, not a diversion.

B) You have chosen to be the owner of a small to medium-sized company that works with the larger company. You may be making less money personally than the executive hosting the suite, but you are, in essence the owner of your own ship. You have final authority on all decisions that involve your company, a power that the executive does not have. The fate of all your employees rests on your shoulders, and this is a heavy responsibility, but one that you cheerfully bear. No matter what the disparity between your paycheck and that of the executive, you would not trade places with any employees, regardless of what company they worked for.

> Another reason that you are in business for yourself is the freedom factor.

You are supremely self-confident. To a great extent, you control how fast and how far your company expands. Even if the company never grows any larger, at least you will have the satisfaction of knowing that you took your venture as far as you could—basically by yourself.

Sure, the success or failure of your business depends upon you, but you relish this opportunity to show your individual business skills, your Entrepreneurial Spirit, and your courage. While you must work with other companies, and in some cases work for them, you are ultimately in business for yourself.

To a great extent, your business is an extension of yourself. It mirrors your personality and your experience. In most cases, the more you learn and the more you apply your lessons to your business, the stronger the business will become. This is not necessarily true of the intrapreneur, whose skills and choices are often restricted by the company owner.

> Your small business is a family heirloom that you can choose to pass down to your children or grandchildren.

So, entrepreneur, sit back and enjoy the hospitality. At least for this evening, the intrapreneur is working for you.

Evaluate your results

We have come to the end of the test, a small but important part of the journey of the entrepreneur, which continues in the next two chapters. Why not take a few minutes now to review your responses? Examine all 15 entries, preferably one at a time, and then chapter by chapter. Then take a look at the larger picture depicted by all 15 responses. It's a lot of information to assimilate, but once you have done so, I believe that you will have a better impression of yourself and your entrepreneurial personality than when you began. Are you an aggressive risk-taker, committed to creating an empire, or a conservative small-businessperson, content with limited profits and the self-satisfaction that comes from being your own boss? Or are you one of the hundreds of thousands of entrepreneurs who fall somewhere in-between and represent a combination of traits from both extremes?

Your business personality is defined not only by strengths, but also by your weaknesses. Therefore, it's in your best interest to take note of any areas of vulnerability that you might uncover while exploring your responses. Do you

Risks, Goals, and Change

focus too much on details, or not enough? Can you roll with the punches that change and competition dole out, or do you just get punched out? Do you have difficulty managing others? Setting priorities? Confronting problems? Looking at the big picture while you handle the everyday routine? No doubt you've discovered some key areas that need improvement, and believe me, that is a good thing.

All About Money

9

All About Money

> *I believe it is my duty to make money and still more money....*
> —J. D. Rockefeller

Priority One: Making Money

If making money—or becoming "cash flow positive"—is not your initial goal, then any success you achieve will be completely accidental. Without money, you won't be able to attract investors, nor will you be able to operate a viable business, hire competent employees or withstand a slump in the economy. This emphasis upon making money, at least in the beginning, goes hand in hand with making a clear business plan and choosing a product or service that fills an actual need, and therefore has the potential to be profitable. Now, might you also derive satisfaction from becoming an independent business person and perhaps making a positive contribution to society? Of course. But for

> The primary purpose of an entrepreneur starting or taking over a business is to make money.

you, at this point, these objectives are of secondary importance to making a profit.

> Making money is rarely easy.

Fortunately, making money is not an insurmountable goal for the true entrepreneur. When entrepreneurs have made up their minds, very little, if anything, can stop them. They seem to have the ability to turn the impossible into the possible.

I'm reminded of a man I knew who raised mules. "There's something to be said for being what people call 'mule-headed,'" he told me once, when I was visiting his farm. "See that poplar?" He pointed toward a very large shrub—a tree, really, with many slender, interlacing trunks and branches. "Now you could never get a horse or even a dog to go through that mess," the mule-breeder continued. "They would see it as an impenetrable obstacle, and to most animals it would be. But if you ride a mule toward that tangle, he won't question your sanity. He won't calculate the probability of making it through. He won't swerve away and find an easier route or run back to the barn. He'll just barrel right on through, like a Patton tank, whether you manage to stay with him or not. He's just too stubborn to believe he can't make it."

I prefer to believe that the mule simply believes that he can go through the tangled tree, and therefore he does. He's not mule-headed, but, like the best entrepreneurs, he is incredibly focused and self-confident.

Like mules, entrepreneurs don't have any tolerance for the impossible. Likewise, they have little or no tolerance for doomsayers. It's not because they don't listen to a variety of advisors. They do. But they normally choose to hear only that which inspires, motivates and excites them to the possibilities of creating that proverbial "better mousetrap." To build that better mousetrap it takes *money*.

All About Money

The entrepreneur has to have the means to fund his enterprise if his vision is to be realized. Therefore much of his time is spent figuring out the dollars and cents of things. This is why entrepreneurs sometimes appear to be obsessed with money. It really boils down to this: Entrepreneurs must find a way to finance their projects until their product or service has the time to make them money. The money they make from that product or service allows them to continue improving and expanding their business.

Why Play the Game

I'm going to suppose that you do not have rich parents with deep pockets, you haven't won the lottery, nor do you have a bulging savings account. Let's assume that you probably don't have much money left at the end of the day. So to you it may appear that the only way to make money is to have money. That can be a depressing thought and a dangerous one, too. If you believe this, chances are you'll be too paralyzed to make a move.

The prospects for securing financial backing for your new enterprise may not look so good when you read the newspaper or listen to the news about the failure of dot.com companies, in addition to responsible investors, irrational venture capitalists, mass layoffs, darlings of Wall Street in bankruptcy, and class action suits stacked up from here to Eternity. Why would anyone want to get involved in this seemingly confused world? Most wouldn't. But, if you are reading this book, you are not like most people. You probably have:

- An overwhelming desire to create something
- A fairly sharp intellect
- An ability to stay focused on a venture
- The ability to change, bend and modify rules
- The drive to execute a plan

- The need for only one person to give you a pat on the back—yourself
- Time only for meaningful exchange
- A spouse or family member who cheers you on

According to the book *Reading in Financial Planning*, edited by David M. Cordell, you as an entrepreneur also:

- Emphasize merit rather than seniority in job promotions
- Enjoy work that involves decision-making
- Require little time to make a major decision
- Complete tests that have a time limit very quickly, attempting to compensate for making more mistakes by answering more questions
- Take a chance and guess on tests that impose a penalty for guessing
- Are optimistic, seeing mistakes as setbacks, not personal failures
- Have a low need for an ordered environment
- Are able to handle stress
- Are persistent

So, when you look at it as Mr. Cordell does, you have a lot going for you. To what degree? Let's take a look at your financial risk tolerance, which says a lot about your personality and your entrepreneurial skills.

Financial Risk Tolerance

First Rule

Nothing is for free. This is especially true about financing an enterprise, whether the money comes from family, friends, professional investors or a lending institution. In order to get something, you'll have to give something in return.

All About Money

Second Rule

Ask yourself some important questions. Here are some to get you started:

- Why do I want the money?
- How much do I really need?
- How much am I willing to give?
- Is my dream worth the price I'll have to pay?
- What will I do with the money?
- How will I pay it back?
- Where am I on the Monetary Risk Tolerance Scale?

As you answer these questions, be brutally honest with yourself. By avoiding the path of self-deception, you will come to:

- Know your risk tolerance
- Define your comfort level
- Sort out options

Measurement of Your Risk Tolerance Level

It is impossible to avoid risk completely. So we have to define our boundaries, establish our borders, and do the best we can with what we have to work with. Every day you are sizing up situations, people, conditions, and events. In fact, most of the time we react to our perceptions without conscious awareness. In some cases that is a good idea. For example, imagine

> When you really think about it, risk is all around us—in every part of our life.

that you are in the path of a fast moving truck. Are you going to take the time to measure the pros and cons, take distance measurements, weigh the benefits of life and death? Unless you have a death wish, you are going to leap out of the truck's path as fast as you can and think about it later.

Just as there are times to react before you consciously think, there are times to consciously think before you act. Borrowing money demands thoughtful, fully conscious thinking.

Basically there are five areas of life in which we encounter risk:

1) Monetary
2) Physical
3) Emotional
4) Social
5) Ethical

Monetary

Monetary risk is a matter of weighing your potential of loss of capital. There are some practical ways of determining monetary risk—market variables, competition, need, cost, etc. You will also need to consider the repercussions of a financial loss, which could include falling deeply in debt, bankruptcy, or even the total loss of your business. When determining your monetary risk level, take a good look at the other four areas of risk, as there is little if anything in life that is not somehow connected to the rest of our world. The degree of the connection for you may vary from those of other people. The intensity may also increase or decrease, depending upon the situation, your experience and your attitude.

Physical

Even if you have a high risk tolerance in all five categories, that doesn't mean that you can climb Everest, go skydiving, bungee jump off a bridge, or participate in a stock car race. Financial risk and physical risk are not related. But, if you stay up nights worrying about an investment you just made, refuse to leave a job you hate because you like the security, and avoid any sort of gamble as if it were the plague, then anything but a sure bet is going to make you physically ill.

Emotional

Do you know the leading cause of divorce? Money. What do most crimes involve? Money. What is most coveted by people? Money. It has been said that money is the root of all evil. I certainly don't believe that in any way, shape or form. Money can't be bad or good. It's only money. It is what people do with or for it that determines good or evil. So, when determining your monetary risk level, take into consideration the emotional impact that the risk will have upon you.

Social

Financial risk affects your social standing as well. However, most entrepreneurs usually possess high self-esteem, have redefined the meaning of failure, and really don't care if they lose the respect of people who don't understand what it means to be an entrepreneur. Therefore, entrepreneurs are probably least vulnerable in this area. Even if social standing is important to them, financial loss usually doesn't affect them as deeply as it does other people. If they suffer a setback and can no longer pay for the luxurious lifestyle they have grown accustomed to, they view this only as a temporary situation. Another promising venture is already stirring inside their minds. On the other hand, while material loss means little to them, entrepreneurs hate to lose the respect of someone they admire, and will do just about anything to avoid this.

Ethical

There are three distinct parts to ethical risk tolerance:

1) A personal standard
2) A religious standard
3) A legal standard

The second and third standards are easier to comprehend than the first. Churches have doctrines, societies have laws, and all are written down for everyone to read. They are more or less tangible and predictable, despite the many interpretations of laws, statutes, ordinances, and cannons.

Religious and legal standards have evolved over a long period of time. They have been tested, proven, changed and amended. If you don't uphold a religious or moral doctrine, you can make a confession, do penance, make atonement, pray or seek spiritual guidance. You can even leave that particular religious organization for another, or form your own church, as Martin Luther and John Knox did. If you break society's laws, you could lose your freedom, even forfeit your life, depending upon the crime and the degree of your punishment.

But individual ethical standards are different. They are never written down and codified, unless you decide to do it. There is no obvious penalty if you violate your individual code of ethical behavior unless, of course, your actions conflict with established religious or legal codes.

> To me, the discussion of the individual standard is rather like a climb up a very steep and slippery slope.

People far more educated than I have come up with what they believe an individual's standards should be, but you are not legally bound to choose them. You can philosophize,

All About Money

suggest, demand, list and insist all you want, but a person's Individual Standard of ethical behavior is personal, based upon his or her own experiences, decisions, desires and goals.

Not everyone will live up to your personal standards, of course. Someone once told me, "The problem with you, Mel, is that you have your own set of individual standards and ideas, and you expect the rest of the world to live up to those standards. Life doesn't work that way. You must remember that those are your standards, not necessarily those of everyone else." This person was right, but I still think that it is necessary to create your own standards and remain true to them. If nothing else, people will admire you for your consistency and the courage of your convictions.

How you or I come up with our own Individual Standard is a matter of speculation. Are we born a certain way? Do our parents determine our personal standards? Is one's brain wired differently from any other person's? Does education, experience, or environment determine our standards? Maybe it's a combination of all of the above. Can anyone really know for sure?

An entrepreneur whom I'll call Sally told me this story about her first defining moment in business. She had started her company with $3,000 she had borrowed from a relative and, as she tells it, "I busted my back working day and night to stay in business." Shortly after her one-year anniversary, she was approached by a couple of investors who offered her two million dollars to help her business grow. She listened to their proposal, then had her lawyer check the legal aspects. Everything was in order. Still, she felt dissatisfied. Something didn't feel right about the deal. So, she called up a retired attorney, whom she had adopted as her mentor.

"I know it doesn't make business sense to turn down this opportunity," she explained to him. "But I don't like the investors. I only like their money. What should I do?"

His answer was brilliant. "If you read about your actions in tomorrow's paper, could you live with them? If something makes you feel ashamed or embarrassed, or is not in keeping with your own set of standards, then don't do it."

She turned down the money.

I asked her why she made that decision.

"I figured that, if I didn't like them, there was something about them not to like. I trusted my feelings. My moral compass didn't want me to enter into an arrangement with them, and I couldn't have lived with myself if I did."

Nearly 15 years have passed since Sally made that decision. When I asked her if she thought, in hindsight, that she made the right decision, she showed no hesitation. "Yes," she answered, then quickly added, "Believe me, there were times when I thought that this was the single most stupid decision I ever made. But I realize now that I would have lost my business to them. I was too inexperienced, and they were too savvy. One day I would have woken up powerless, and they would have been in control of my company."

I asked her what she would do today if those same two investors showed up at her doorstep with the same proposal. "Heck, I'd love to have their money," Sally said. "But I know these guys. I know their true intentions, and I know mine. So I'd have to decline the offer again."

Sometimes, you make a decision based upon what seemed like sound and pragmatic reasons, but in hindsight, you realize that your judgment was colored by not only who you were at that time, but also not truly being honest with yourself.

When I left the wholesale tobacco business to acquire vending routes, my partners and I became very successful very quickly and became one of the largest independent operators in the United States. I was then approached by a large public company who wanted to purchase our company and offered me a senior executive position and a seat on the Board of Directors. I was flattered and convinced myself that I could do things on a bigger and better scale and prove to the world what a talented businessman I had become. After two stormy years, I left the company and repurchased one of the routes I had sold. As I matured as a businessman and learned about my inner feelings, I realized I had made a mistake in selling not because of the logical reasons, but because I did not truly understand my own need to be an entrepreneur.

Other Determining Factors

Several other factors affect our levels of risk tolerance:

- Education
- Age
- Gender
- Birth Order
- Marital Status
- Occupation

Men are more risk tolerant in all areas. However, entrepreneurship is one area where one's sex does not matter. Those first in the birth order are less inclined to take risks than later-born siblings. Single people are willing to risk more than married people. And, finally, the

> Recent studies show that your tolerance to financial risk increases with the amount of formal education you receive but decreases with age.

Entrepreneur Made E-Z

type of job you hold tells a lot about your risk tolerance in general. But, when all is said and done, risk tolerance comes down to the wisdom of Socrates, who admonished his students to remember only one dictum: *Know thyself.*

Hopefully, the test you took earlier in this book has helped you gauge your abilities as an entrepreneur, as well as your level of risk tolerance and your basic personality traits. This should help you know yourself, or at least your goals, a little better.

Financing Your Enterprise

10

Financing Your Enterprise 10

You never want to put yourself in a position of obtaining money that you are unable to repay.
—The Author

So far, we've examined risk, engaged in some personal mapping, and discussed tolerance levels. At this point, you're probably saying to yourself, "It's time to make some money." That's all well and good, but before you can make money, you must have funds to invest in your business. How do you intend to get those funds? It's not very likely that investors will approach you to offer you funding. So finding funding is up to you. But whom should you contact for funding? What are you going to say to them? How are you going to say it? In this chapter, we're going to address those questions and investigate some potential ways to generate money.

The dreaded business plan

A workable business plan can lead to securing funding and is, therefore, a necessary topic for our discussion. Since

Entrepreneurship Made E-Z

there are many books written on the subject, I am not going to go into much detail here. Examples of well-written business plans that have raised capital are readily accessible in books and on the Internet.

Writing a business plan is about as much fun to an entrepreneur as writing a thesis is to a doctoral candidate. But it must be done. And it should be done. Why? Besides the fact that bankers and investors require one, writing a business plan gives you a wonderful opportunity to figure out how your own business operates. It helps you define your own vision for your enterprise, gives you a plan of action and clarifies and refines your concept. Besides, if you are starting a brand new business, putting together a business plan shouldn't take more than a few weeks. (An existing business will take longer, since you will have to take into account the years of operation that took place before you came on board.)

Whether you are starting a new venture or taking over an existing business, you must show how you are going to make money, what the source of funding will be and how you will pay back the money you have borrowed. Obtaining answers to these questions will help determine whom you are going to approach for funding in the first place.

> Unlike large companies and corporations, the new entrepreneur normally doesn't have the luxury of money, time and personnel that he can use when creating a business plan.

Once you do some preliminary work on your business plan and determine the amount of money that you will need, the sources of that money will become much more apparent to you. It is very important to know who your potential investors will be, since all investors have a different

Financing Your Enterprise

> Whom you approach for funding has a great deal to do with how you are going to raise the money.

outlook on the money that they put into a business. Some are simply concerned with making a high return on their investment in capital appreciation, while others want interest income. Others are specifically looking to invest in businesses run by people of a certain age, background or ethnic group, and are less interested in huge, fast profits than they are in supporting that interest group.

Structuring a business plan

The most important thing to realize when writing a business plan is that investors are not going to spend a lot of time reading it. They want to find out who's in charge, what the business is all about, and what they can expect to get for their money. Therefore, it is important to keep your plan simple yet effective. Once you determine who your potential investors are, as well as their needs and expectations, you'll want to tell them *why* you believe that you are going to be successful in this business and *how* you intend to become successful. If this sounds like an easy task, let me assure you that it is not, and you will probably have to go through several drafts before the plan is as simple and straightforward as you want it to be.

Different ventures demand different business plans. For example, if you are proposing to manufacture a new medical instrument, you should include an abbreviated version of the blueprint design. The key is to remember that you are writing a business plan for a specific audience, so you must be aware of their needs. *Winning Busines Plans Made E-Z*, available through Made E-Z Products,® Inc. provides a good model analysis.

187

The following sections are always included in a business plan:

- Mission Statement
- Market Analysis
- Sales and Marketing Strategy
- Executive Summary
- Projection of Revenues
- Product or Service Strategy
- Management Personnel
- Financial Plan
- Exit Plan

See the Appendix for an example of the Table of Contents of a formal and detailed business proposal, in this case regarding the development, manufacturing, marketing and distribution of a breakthrough medical device.

Executive Summary and Financial Plan

The two most important sections of a business plan are the Executive Summary and the Financial Plan. While business plans are normally not read word for word by interested parties, these two areas are carefully scrutinized. The Executive Summary is your opportunity to intrigue your potential investor with your idea. It shouldn't be too lengthy, since you don't want to risk boring your reader. Keep it to between three and five pages. The Financial Plan is about numbers. Include financial projections and new capital that you require.

Financing the enterprise

There is probably no harder decision you will have to make than how to finance your venture. The only words of reassurance that I have for you is that it will help prepare

Financing Your Enterprise

you for the other hard decisions you will have to make as an entrepreneur. And there will be plenty.

We already established that your paycheck is just getting you by. Still, you are committed to your dream. Now is the time to survey your options. Again, there are many books available that detail funding sources, so I'll just introduce, or re-introduce, as the case may be, some avenues to consider. They are as follows:

- Family and Friends
- Professional Investors
- Private Investors
- Customer Financing
- Small Business Administration Loans (SBA)
- Bank Financing
- Venture Capitalists
- Initial Public Offerings
- Customer Financing
- Founder Assets

A word about investors

Entrepreneurs are in love with their ideas. They have to be if they have any chance of making their dreams a reality. But investors would rather invest in a product than an idea. Investors like to see services that are operational, track records, and customer demographics. If all you have to present to investors is an idea, it had better be well-thought-out, and even then securing funding is going to be almost impossible. Therefore, you may have to get your enterprise to the stage where it is operational before approaching investors.

Let's suppose for a moment that you did find an investor for your idea. You may think yourself lucky and feel as if you just hit the jackpot. But when all you have is an idea, the trade-off is going be very high. The investor will probably want a substantial return for his or her risk, a circumstance that will narrow your margin for success. Why? Because you may find yourself working for the investor instead of working at implementing your vision.

In my opinion, one of the first mistakes that novice entrepreneurs make is believing that an investor is the golden goose who will provide for them. I often wonder why they would have this belief. Most things in life just are not that easy. Why should business implementation be any different?

The second mistake new entrepreneurs make is to approach investors before they are ready to do so. This leads to rejection, and subsequently a huge letdown. So it is normally best to be armed with the following before seeking an investor:

- Existing products or services
- A functional business
- Paying customers
- Management team
- A business plan

Banks and SBA loans

When borrowing money from a bank or the Small Business Administration (SBA), it's good to know up front that:

- You have to guarantee how, when and how much gets paid back.
- Hopefully you have some collateral; it may be required.

Financing Your Enterprise

- You will have to fill out a lot of paperwork, more so with the SBA.
- Bank loans are usually shorter in term than SBA loans.

There's no use in complaining that banks tend to loan money to people who don't need it. They're in business, and they don't like excessive risk any more than you do. But if you do secure a loan from a bank and you pay it back, they'll want you to borrow more from them. Having this option can provide peace of mind. At least you know that you do have access to money if the need should arise.

Basically, you should remember that there are three C's to lending money:

- Character
- Capital
- Capacity

Of these, character is the most important. Often it is the integrity of a person that is the tipping point for lenders. Honesty, sincerity, thoughtfulness and fairness are all marks in your favor,

> Relatives, friends, customers, banks and investors don't lend you money just because they like your business plan.

and the investor will look for these. Decent people finish first on many levels.

I know an individual—I'll call him Tyrone—who had made a move from being an intrapreneur to becoming an entrepreneur. Tyrone had reached a crisis point in his finances where there was much more money going out than coming in. He had borrowed, mortgaged and re-mortgaged all he could. Creditors were all over him. A friend who worked at the bank and knew of his problems pulled him aside and suggested bankruptcy as an option. Tyrone thought about it, then came up with this *plan for survival* instead:

- Renegotiating terms of loans
- Selling the business
- Contacting creditors

To make a long story short, Tyrone decided not to claim bankruptcy, yet he made good on all of his commitments, and did not have to sell his business. Eventually, the business began to turn a profit. As a result of demonstrating the strength of his character to his lenders, Tyrone enjoyed a long-term relationship with his lending institution. Over the years, he was able to secure financial support, even when his collateral and ability to pay back the loan were not as "healthy" as the lender would have liked.

Venture capitalists

A venture capitalist not only lends funds to you to proceed with your plans for your business, he owns shares of your business. This may seem innocent enough, but keep this in mind: If he accumulates enough shares, he can take over your business, and you may be in a position of working for someone else, not for yourself.

> Before signing on with a venture capitalist investigate the option very carefully and make certain that you understand what you are agreeing to. Do not allow the dollars offered to cloud your judgment.

A word of caution: Venture capital should be sought by sophisticated entrepreneurs guided by sound legal advice. The less experienced entrepreneur is likely to run into problems comprehending the value of venture capital versus its true cost.

Founder assets

Using founder assets is normally the way that most new entrepreneurs have to finance their businesses, at least in the beginning. Why? Well, let's change hats for a moment.

You are the investor. A person called Lester comes to you with a business plan and a good idea. In the course of the conversation, you learn that Lester has a home with a few years left on the mortgage, a nice retirement package from his job, and money in a savings account. Furthermore, his spouse brings in a respectable income, and he owns a luxury car as well as a little vacation home on the beach. He has no viable business and no customers. Only an idea.

But Lester has obviously not invested in his own idea. Would you invest in a person who hasn't invested in himself? The willingness to invest your money, remortgage your house, borrow from your retirement, your life insurance or other holdings, and sell property to begin your enterprise tells a lot about your commitment level to your idea, your company and your belief in yourself.

> The point here is this: The first source of funding to consider is your own.

Money is not the only consideration when investing in your enterprise. Time is also a factor. You may wish to consider working at a "real" job and use your spare time developing your services or products, defining your business and building a customer base.

There's a lot to be said for building your business on your own terms—using your own resources. Of course, this route normally is not appreciated until you're a success and the battle is won. But it does give you bragging rights. More than that, it shows potential investors that you understand the concept of personal energy versus that of financial energy.

Customer financing

While customers prefer to use suppliers who have a steady and accessible cash flow, customer financing is not uncommon. But it goes without saying that to have customers you must first have a business. Here are a few ways in which customer financing is normally structured:

Pre-payment for goods—This is usually done with new customers who haven't established credit with your company. For example, smaller publishing companies often pay printing companies four to six weeks *before* their books are printed and shipped.

Percentage completion payments—In this arrangement, a company provides long-term services or sales for another company. Basically, payments are collected at intervals as the work is being completed, rather than pre-paying or paying when the service is completed.

Credit for future service—Here, a company (normally a service-oriented company) is paid monies up front, which are then applied to the total cost of services that are provided over a one- or two-year period. An example of this method is the retainer often paid to an attorney.

Debt

I have only one thing to say about it: Get used to it. That may sound a bit flippant, but it's a fact that entrepreneurs know the pressure of writing a check on Friday and covering it on

> Like it or not, there will be times when you find yourself backing up, way back, so you can move forward.

Monday. Take a page from the notebook of Rembrandt, the fabulously famous Dutch artist. In his last years, in utter poverty and in debt up to his eyelashes, he used to give

Financing Your Enterprise

away his paintings in return for just enough money to buy more pigments, oil paints and canvas, so he could go on reaching even higher levels of artistic triumph.

In a strange way, sometimes the amount of debt is an indicator of an individual's strength of character. Take Tyrone for example, again. He showed his integrity by paying back his creditors when bankruptcy was a distinct, even encouraged option.

I'm reminded of Russell, a colleague who managed to build up a vast amount of debt in a very short span of time. Once, when I was out to dinner with him and a mutual friend, I asked Russell how he could have amassed so much debt so quickly. Before Russell could respond, the third party piped up, "He must be very trustworthy." He surely must have been, or he would never have been able to raise the money that he did. (Unfortunately, unlike Russell, there are also plenty of con men who manage to accumulate large amounts of debt without ever intending to pay it back. Don't use them for a role model!)

Being debt-free would be like living in the state of Nirvana. Every once in a while, you'll get a glimpse of that perfect, stress-free state of being in which money is of no concern. When you are there, enjoy the moment. For that's about how long debt-free Nirvana lasts.

The Right Style For You

11

The Right Style For You   11

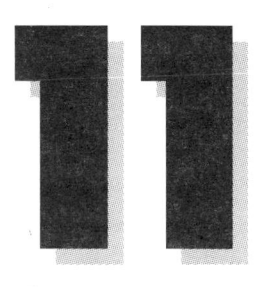

> *Make voyages!—Attempt them!—*
> *There is nothing else.*
> —Tennessee Williams

As with any journey, getting there is most of the fun, and most of the challenge as well. But there are a variety of ways to take this particular journey, which you no doubt know simply

> It has been said that life is a journey, not a destination, and the same can be said of being an entrepreneur.

from taking the test in this book and from observing entrepreneurs you've met or read about. Different entrepreneurs have different styles, and there is no right or wrong way to go into business for yourself on the Entrepreneurial Highway. You'll have a lot of factors to weigh because your journey will be different from that of every other entrepreneur to go before you or after you.

Throughout this book, indirectly, we have discussed and speculated about the various types or styles of entrepreneurs. Therefore it makes sense by way of a summary to try to get a better handle on some of these characters that we have met in the preceding pages. I always think of the life of the entrepreneur as being a highway, and I used the analogy of a "journey" several times in this book. "Traveling" through life and learning about business and one's self seems to be part of the entrepreneurial experience. Here are the different kinds of travelers that I have encountered on the Entrepreneurial Highway:

- The Speedster
- The Cruiser
- The Van Owner
- The Parallel Driver
- The Car Owner

Let's take a closer look at them. Maybe you'll even find yourself among them.

The Speedster

This is the inventor or innovator, the entrepreneur so focused on the horizon before him or her that he or she can see nothing else. To him or her, the journey is an agenda of goals, which he or she intends to meet, one after the other, or all at once, if he or she can.

The Speedster has built his or her own vehicle—a product, service, or combination of both—and he or she has a great deal of faith in it. If it fails him or her, or if he or she takes it as far as he or she thinks it will go, he or she will create another and forsake the first. Don't leave your own vehicle unguarded on the roadside. The Speedster might "borrow" a part of it, making it less effective or even undriveable. He or she might even try to buy your vehicle—not to drive it, but to salvage parts from it to improve his or her own.

The Right Style For You

Speed is important to the Speedster. He or she is not in a race, but he or she drives as if he or she were in one. His or her aim is to be faster, bigger, better and more attractive than any other driver. But sometimes, despite his or her ambition, talent and desires, his or her unique vehicle breaks down along the road. Like Colonel Sander's stop/start career, that vehicle may break down many times, often in spite of the entrepreneur's skill and wisdom. Strikes, fires, litigation, regulations—they can limit the freedom of the most aggressive entrepreneur, and they can slow him or her down, or even stop his or her progress.

Take Bill Gates, for example. A brilliant and extremely focused innovator, Gates was "pulled aside" by the Federal Government when his company, Microsoft, was deemed to be in violation of Federal legislation against monopolies. Gates prevailed, however, and was soon back on the road. Granted, Microsoft was a changed company, and his competitors now had a chance to catch up with him and even surpass him, but his influence in the world of computer technology was so great that he simply could not be derailed altogether.

> **The Speedster is more likely than any other entrepreneur to take the biggest calculated risks.**

Gates, for instance, risked creating a monopoly and even losing his company because of it. But the true innovator knows that the greatest risks can produce the greatest gains. As fearless as he or she is focused, the Speedster tends to venture where others fear to go. But when he or she looks over his or her shoulder, he or she'll see that a throng of competitors are right behind him or her. And he or she loves it.

The Speedster would much prefer to drive his or her vehicle all the time and monitor every aspect of his or her business; however, he or she is savvy enough to know that this isn't possible. He or she can't control every aspect of his or her enterprise and must rely on competent assistance, especially as the business grows.

Words that describe the Speedster personality— intelligent, insightful, innovative, highly risk tolerant, competitive, knowledgeable of industry, supremely self-confident, good negotiator, motivated, focused, and driven.

The Cruiser

He or she hasn't invented his or her vehicle, but he or she has souped it up for a specific purpose. The Cruiser is an *implementer*. While he or she may not come up with brilliant concepts, he or she can apply someone else's idea or product to his or her own venture and make the result his or her own.

> The Cruiser is a crowd pleaser.

He or she actively seeks an audience for his or her product or service, and he or she'll do wheelies and other stunts—whatever is necessary—to grow his or her market. His or her skill is adapting another person's idea to a new market or application. Dave Thomas of Wendy's Restaurants and David Oreck of Oreck Vacuums are both examples of Cruisers. It is as if they had driven their vehicles up to the summit of a tall mesa overlooking the route of the Speedster, and watched him or her as he or she sped past. Perhaps the Speedster's unique spoiler caught their eye, or maybe the jet propulsion units affixed to his or her oddly effective roadster. Whatever the innovation, the Cruiser can probably find a way to put it to use in his or her business, in ways that improve upon the original.

The Cruiser will also take the bigger risks, but of course not the most dangerous ones. He or she's always on the lookout for ways to make himself or herself competitive

The Right Style For You

with the Speedster, and he or she knows he or she will have to sacrifice some element of safety in order to reach those high speeds and cruise those long distances. Oh, he or she's had his or her share of crashes, too, and sometimes they are just as spectacular as the Speedster's. Think of Zayre's, Hill's, Ames, K-Mart and other discount department stores that tried to make a unique appeal to the market and either failed or did not meet their expectations. Then there are those who succeeded, such as Target Department Stores, by narrowing their market niche and appealing to higher-end consumers. Leave it to The Cruiser to take a carefully calculated risk and fine-tune it into a success.

The Cruiser knows he or she can't handle his or her sprawling vehicle all by himself or herself, even though he or she actually might be able to do so for a short while. He or she's so devoted to his or her business that he or she'd clean the toilets if he or she had to. He or she is thoughtful, thorough and careful when it comes to delegating tasks.

Words that describe The Cruiser—Involved at all levels, inspiring, risk tolerant, resourceful, flexible, intelligent, "street smart," responsible, and responsive.

The Van Owner

This entrepreneur loves to share his or her ride. He or she loves being with other people, and is always inviting others—partners, associates, employees, consultants, investors, advertisers—to hop on board. Perhaps he or she owns a medium to large business with a sizeable staff, or perhaps he or she is a partner in a large, successful law firm. He or she doesn't mind competition; in fact, he or she welcomes it. He or she'll race his or her van against anyone. Sometimes he or she drives, but at other times he or she may allow others to control his or her vehicle. He or she has no difficulty delegating responsibilities, but he or she may have some trouble monitoring all his or her helpers and their tasks.

The Van Owner takes lots of detours, as his or her "passengers" stop to visit roadside attractions. He or she may take on more responsibility than he or she can handle—too many stores, too many employees, too much expansion happening too quickly—but he or she is usually sharp enough to get his or her venture turned around and back on the road, headed in the right direction.

The Van Owner isn't interested in great speed. He or she'll take as long as he or she needs to reach a goal, especially if he or she is in his or her element, surrounded by other people. He or she wants to make the world a better place, to contribute to society in some way, but he or she probably won't risk his or her comfort and security in order to do so. He or she does run a risk that his or her passengers will become freeloaders—that is, he or she may treat his or her employees like family and keep them on whether they are effective workers or not. In any case, he or she isn't likely to search out the high risks. He or she's enjoying his or her journey too much.

Words that describe The Van Owner—Knowledgeable in industry, intelligent, competitive, willing to take some risks, basic skills in finance and marketing, minimum skills in employee relations, committed, and cautious.

The Parallel Driver

The Parallel Driver, hasn't quite committed to the Entrepreneurial Highway, but he or she admires it from a distance and even emulates its drivers, driving along beside them on a separate, adjoining road.

> Access roads often parallel large highways, and this is where you will find The Parallel Driver, or Intrapreneur.

An intrapreneur is like an entrepreneur who works for someone else. Thus, in the strictest sense of the word, he or

The Right Style For You

she is not really an entrepreneur. Nevertheless, he or she exhibits many traits of the entrepreneur, even the most driven, aggressive entrepreneurs. He or she'll take the big risks and make the big investments—but he or she'll do so using money that belongs to someone else. He or she may be extremely devoted to the business, and work long, hard and faithfully to steer it in the right direction and make it a success. However, no matter how diligent his or her efforts, the business is not his or her, and he or she is not likely to get much credit for a job well done.

Therefore, The Parallel Driver tools along beside the entrepreneurs, imitating their ventures, perhaps, but not taking part in a business of his or her own. Now, the parallel road does connect with the Entrepreneurial Highway from time to time, and the Intrapreneur has the opportunity to take that on ramp and drive on the Highway. Being an intrapreneur is excellent preparation for going into business for yourself and learning all the skills you'll need to do so. Nevertheless, the intrapreneur doesn't tend to stay long on the Entrepreneurial Highway—unless he or she has made so much money that he or she can continue being an entrepreneur without real financial risk to his or her net worth. In that case, he or she will probably resemble a Speedster or a Cruiser.

Interestingly enough, some entrepreneurs have exited the Highway to travel the intrapreneur's road, but usually not for very long. Perhaps their business has been bought out by a larger one, and they have gone to work for their competitor. Or perhaps they are well aware that they lack some important skill or experience that they can easily acquire while working for an employer. Chances are, though, they will go back to work for themselves at the first opportunity they get. If you truly have the Entrepreneurial Spirit, you will always hunger to work independently, to take your own risks, make your own mistakes, and find your own successes.

Entrepreneurship Made E-Z

Words that describe The Parallel Driver—Intelligent, insightful, cautious, devoted, knowledgeable of industry, not inspiring to others, less than fully self-confident, risk-adverse, and hesitant.

The Car Owner

The Car Owner loves his or her car. More specifically, he or she loves having his or her own car, no matter how small or inefficient or conventional it may be. And if it is a Toyota Celica, and 90% of the other drivers are driving one, too, no problem.

> To be independent—to be in charge of his or her own destiny—is one of this entrepreneur's chief goals.

The Car Owner typically drives alone. He or she may take on an assistant to help with the driving, but only if he or she feels that this is really necessary. He or she isn't looking for anyone to take his or her place, because, as far as he or she is concerned, he or she's going solo. That's what he or she enjoys most about his or her trip down the highway, the fact that he or she is his or her own boss. He or she may take very few risks or even be risk adverse, because he or she does not want to jeopardize the business that he or she has developed and, to some extent, represents him or her as an individual.

If you are a Car Owner, you might own your own small business, or you might be a consultant for other companies. You might be an actor, writer or other artist, or an athlete or musician or other person with a highly developed skill. Perhaps you are a dentist or doctor or lawyer with a small practice, or a chiropractor or physical therapist. Maybe you run a lawn-care business, or operate a daycare facility out of your home, or perhaps you are a salesperson working on commission only. Car Owners come in many shapes and sizes, and wealth is usually much less important to them

The Right Style For You

than independence. On the other hand, some Car Owners are among the wealthiest, most successful entrepreneurs around.

Words that describe The Car Owner—Independent, resourceful, dedicated, hard-working, intelligent, highly skilled in one narrow area, determined, persevering, somewhat limited in industry knowledge or a range of skills, cautious, and risk-adverse.

A few final words

Now we really are at the end of the road, literally and figuratively. Therefore, it only seems natural to come full circle. Here's a question that I asked very early on our voyage together: Are entrepreneurs born or made? My answer was that they are both. I would rather work with someone who has the passion to succeed than a very talented deadbeat. There are numerous examples of people who are extremely talented yet have wasted their talent because they have not nurtured the gift they were given. Likewise, there are thousands of examples of people who took a tiny seed of skill or ability, planted it, cared for it and ended up with a bountiful harvest.

> The amount of talent you are born with will only carry you so far without hard work, education, experience, desire and the like.

No matter how you travel the Entrepreneurial Highway, or whether the E-Fever rages within you or just makes you a little woozy, when all is said and done, it is you who determines what to make from your own business. And, when you think about it, an entrepreneur would not have it any other way. After all, where would the challenge be if entrepreneurs were only born, not made?

I'd like to leave you with these final suggestions as you prepare to pull onto the Entrepreneurial Highway:

1) Attempt to know yourself honestly and fairly. Know your entrepreneurial style, your strengths and weaknesses.
2) Motivate yourself to improve your skills and aspirations, or find someone to help motivate you.
3) Assess risk as it applies to you, your finances and abilities.
4) Avoid the common errors and pitfalls in starting up, taking over and operating a business.
5) Remember that business is about making money. Sales and collections are both of great importance.
6) Regularly evaluate what you are doing on a daily basis and align the results with your goals.
7) If you plan to enter a new business, first try to get a mentor, or work in the field.
8) If you decide to take a chance, be realistic about the capital you will need and the time it will take to become "cash flow positive."
9) If your business does not allow you to act ethically, morally, and honestly, abandon it. It's not worth doing.
10) Enjoy what you do and be optimistic about the future. This, more than anything else, may be the single most valuable suggestion I can give you.

Good luck, and happy traveling!

Appendix

Example of Business Plan Table of Contents

Section One: Executive Summary
    Key words
    Objective
    Motivation
    Approach
    Patent
    Overview of Plan and Project Needs
    Benefits
    The Overall Strategy
    Benefits
    Data Collection Methodology

Section Two: Products and Services
    Description of Instrument
    The Long-Term Plan
    Need for Development
    History of Instrument
    Early Support
    Need For Critical Support
    Ten Drawbacks to Modern Day Endoscopic and
        Laparascopic Devices

Section Three: Market Analysis and Marketing Strategy
    Customer Base
    Market Awareness
    Market Size
    Distribution
    Product Pricing
    Estimated Revenue

Section Four: Competition: Characterization and Strengths
    Competitors
    Product Mixing

Entrepreneurship Made E-Z

Section Five: Production and Operation Plans
    Location:
    Facility Layout
    Management Personnel

Section Six: Project Goals and Timelines
    Task One
    Task Two
    Task Three
    Task Four
    Tangible Deliverables

Section Seven: Financial Statement and Plans
    Capital Requirements and Proposed Basic Capital Structure
    Projected Breakdown Analysis
    Project Financial Analysis
    Estimated Total Medical Procedures in First Five Years
    Projected Company Sales First Five Years
    Estimated Cost of Goods Sold First Five Years
    Projected Gross Profit First Five Years
    Projected Gross Profit Margin First Five Years

Section Eight: Impact on Community
    Analysis
    Index:

Section Nine: Exhibits

Section Ten: Patient Information

Section Eleven: Selected Recommendations

Resources

••• Online Resources •••

- About.com
  http://www.sbinformation.about.com
- American Entrepreneurs for Economic Growth
  http://www.aeeg.com/
- Business Success Center
  http://www.grow-biz.com/
- Bizmoonlighter.com
  http://www.bizmoonlighter.com
- BizMove.com
  http://www.bizmove.com
- Biztalk.com Small Business Community
  http://www.biztalk.com
- Bplans.com!
  http://www.bplans.com
- Businesspartners.com
  http://www.businesspartners.com/
- BusinessTown.Com
  http://www.businesstown.com
- Council of Better Business Bureaus, Inc.
  http://www.bbb.org
- Education Index, Business Resources
  http://www.educationindex.com/bus
- Entrepreneur's Help Page, The
  http://www.tannedfeet.com/
- Entrepreneur Education Resources
  http://eweb.slu.edu/Default.htm

- ◆ EntrepreneurMag.com
  http://www.entrepreneurmag.com
- ◆ Entrepreneur.com
  http://www.entrepreneur.com/Magazines/MA_FrontDoor/0,4430,,00.html
- ◆ Entreworld.org
  http://www.entreworld.org
- ◆ Federal Trade Commission-Franchise and Business Opportunities
  http://www.ftc.gov/bcp/menu-fran.htm
- ◆ Forum for Women Entrepreneurs
  http://www.fwe.org/p/simple.asp?mlid=66
- ◆ Freewell.com
  http://www.freewell.com/free/Free_Entrepreneurs/
- ◆ FundingPost.com
  http://www.fundingpost.com/index.asp?refer=searchspr
- ◆ Google Web Directory—Resources for Entrepreneurs
  http://directory.google.com/Top/Business/Venture_Capital/Resources_for_Entrepreneurs/
- ◆ Inc. Online
  http://www.inc.com
- ◆ Internal Revenue Service
  http://www.irs.ustreas.gov/prod/cover.html
- ◆ International Finance & Commodities Institute
  http://finance.wat.ch/IFCI
- ◆ Limited Liability Company Website
  http://www.llcweb.com
- ◆ Minority Business Entrepreneur
  http://www.mbemag.com/
- ◆ Moneyhaven
  http://www.moneyhaven.net/

Resources

- National Association of Small Business Investment Companies
  http://www.nasbic.org
- National Foundation for Women Business Owners (NFWBO)
  http://www.nfwbo.org
- National Small Business Development Center (SBDC) Research Network
  http://www.smallbiz.suny.edu
- National Small Business Network Resource Directory
  http://businessknowhow.net/Directory/bkhDindex.asp
- National Small Business United
  http://www.nsbu.org
- North American Securities Administrators Association (NASAA)
  http://www.nasaa.org
- Occupational Safety and Health Administration (OSHA)
  http://www.osha.gov
- Service Core of Retired Executives
  http://www.score.org
- Small Business Administration
  http://www.sba.gov/
- Small Business Advisor
  http://www.isquare.com
- Small Business Primer
  http://www.ces.ncsu.edu/depts/fcs/business/welcome.html
- Small Business Taxes & Management
  http://www.smbiz.com
- Tax and Accounting Sites Directory
  http://www.taxsites.com

Entrepreneurship Made E-Z

- U.S. Business Advisor
  http://www.business.gov
- U.S. Equal Employment Opportunity Commission's (EEOC)
  http://www.eeoc.gov
- U.S. Small Business Administration
  http://www.sbaonline.sba.gov
- U.S. Treasury Department-Business Services
  http://www.ustreas.gov/index.html
- Vfinance.com
  http://www.vfinance.com/
- Wall Street Journal Startup
  http://www.startupjournal.com/
- Webcrawler: Small Business
  http://quicken.webcrawler.com/small_business
- Yahoo! Small Business
  http://smallbusiness.yahoo.com

••• Legal Search Engines •••

- All Law
  http://www.alllaw.com
- American Law Sources On Line
  http://www.lawsource.com/also/cgi?src
- Catalaw
  http://www.catalaw.com
- FindLaw
  http://www.findlaw.com
- InternetOracle
  http://www.internetoracle.com/legal.htm

Resources

- **LawAid**
  http://www.lawaid.com/search.html
- **LawCrawler**
  http://www.lawcrawler.com
- **LawRunner**
  http://www.lawrunner.com
- **'Lectric Law Library**™
  http://www.lectlaw.com
- **Legal Search Engines**
  http://www.dreamscape.com/frankvad/search.legal.html
- **LEXIS/NEXIS Communications Center**
  http://www.lexis-nexis.com
- **Meta-Index for U.S. Legal Research**
  http://gsulaw.gsu.edu/metaindex
- **USALaw**
  http://www.usalaw.com/linksrch.cfm
- **WestLaw**
  http://web2.westlaw.co,/signon/default.wl
  (Registered users only. Fee paid service.)

••• State Bar Associations •••

ALABAMA
Alabama State Bar
415 Dexter Avenue
Montgomery, AL 36104
mailing address:
PO Box 671
Montgomery, AL 36101
(334) 269-1515
http://www.alabar.org

ALASKA
Alaska Bar Association
510 L Street No. 602
Anchorage, AK 99501
mailing address:
PO Box 100279
Anchorage, AK 99510
http://www.alaskabar.org

ARIZONA
State Bar of Arizona
111 West Monroe
Phoenix, AZ 85003-1742
(602) 252-4804
http://www.azbar.org

ARKANSAS
Arkansas Bar Association
400 West Markham
Little Rock, AR 72201
(501) 375-4605
http://www.arkbar.org

CALIFORNIA
State Bar of California
555 Franklin Street
San Francisco, CA 94102
(415) 561-8200
http://www.calbar.org
Alameda County Bar Association
http://www.acbanet.org

COLORADO
Colorado Bar Association
No. 950, 1900 Grant Street
Denver, CO 80203
(303) 860-1115
http://www.cobar.org

CONNECTICUT
Connecticut Bar Association
101 Corporate Place
Rocky Hill, CT 06067-1894
(203) 721-0025
http://www.ctbar.org

DELAWARE
Delaware State Bar Association
1225 King Street, 10th floor
Wilmington, DE 19801
(302) 658-5279
(302) 658-5278 (lawyer referral service)
http://www.dsba.org

DISTRICT OF COLUMBIA
District of Columbia Bar
1250 H Street, NW, 6th Floor
Washington, DC 20005
(202) 737-4700

Resources

Bar Association of the District of Columbia
1819 H Street, NW, 12th floor
Washington, DC 20006-3690
(202) 223-6600
http://www.badc.org

FLORIDA

The Florida Bar
The Florida Bar Center
650 Apalachee Parkway
Tallahassee, FL 32399-2300
(850) 561-5600
http://www.flabar.org

GEORGIA

State Bar of Georgia
800 The Hurt Building
50 Hurt Plaza
Atlanta, GA 30303
(404) 527-8700
http://www.gabar.org

HAWAII

Hawaii State Bar Association
1136 Union Mall
Penthouse 1
Honolulu, HI 96813
(808) 537-1868
http://www.hsba.org

IDAHO

Idaho State Bar
PO Box 895
Boise, ID 83701
(208) 334-4500
http://www2.state.id.us/isb

ILLINOIS

Illinois State Bar Association
424 South Second Street
Springfield, IL 62701
(217) 525-1760
http://www.illinoisbar.org

INDIANA

Indiana State Bar Association
230 East Ohio Street
Indianapolis, IN 46204
(317) 639-5465
http://www.ai.org/isba

IOWA

Iowa State Bar Association
521 East Locust
Des Moines, IA 50309
(515) 243-3179
http://www.iowabar.org

KANSAS

Kansas Bar Association
1200 Harrison Street
Topeka, KS 66612-1806
(785) 234-5696
http://www.ksbar.org

KENTUCKY

Kentucky Bar Association
514 West Main Street
Frankfort, KY 40601-1883
(502) 564-3795
http://www.kybar.org

LOUISIANA

Louisiana State Bar Association
601 St. Charles Avenue
New Orleans, LA 70130
(504) 566-1600
http://www.lsba.org

MAINE
Maine State Bar Association
124 State Street
PO Box 788
Augusta, ME 04330
(207) 622-7523
http://www.mainebar.org

MARYLAND
Maryland State Bar Association
520 West Fayette Street
Baltimore, MD 21201
(301) 685-7878
http://www.msba.org/msba

MASSACHUSETTS
Massachusetts Bar Association
20 West Street
Boston, MA 02111
(617) 542-3602
(617) 542-9103 (lawyer referral service)
http://www.massbar.org

MICHIGAN
State Bar of Michigan
306 Townsend Street
Lansing, MI 48933-2083
(517) 372-9030
http://www.michbar.org

MINNESOTA
Minnesota State Bar Association
514 Nicollet Mall
Minneapolis, MN 55402
(612) 333-1183
http://www.mnbar.org

MISSISSIPPI
The Mississippi Bar
643 No. State Street
Jackson, Mississippi 39202
(601) 948-4471
http://www.msbar.org

MISSOURI
The Missouri Bar
P.O. Box 119, 326 Monroe
Jefferson City, Missouri 65102
(314) 635-4128
http://www.mobar.org

MONTANA
State Bar of Montana
46 North Main
PO Box 577
Helena, MT 59624
(406) 442-7660
http://www.montanabar.org

NEBRASKA
Nebraska State Bar Association
635 South 14th Street, 2nd floor
Lincoln, NE 68508
(402) 475-7091
http://www.nebar.com

NEVADA
State Bar of Nevada
201 Las Vegas Blvd.
Las Vegas, NV 89101
(702) 382-2200
http://www.nvbar.org

Resources

NEW HAMPSHIRE
New Hampshire Bar Association
112 Pleasant Street
Concord, NH 03301
(603) 224-6942
http://www.nhbar.org

NEW JERSEY
New Jersey State Bar Association
One Constitution Square
New Brunswick, NJ 08901-1500
(908) 249-5000

NEW MEXICO
State Bar of New Mexico
5121 Masthead N.E.
Albuquerque, NM 87125
mailing address:
PO Box 25883
Albuquerque, NM 87125
(505) 843-6132
http://www.nmbar.org

NEW YORK
New York State Bar Association
One Elk Street
Albany, NY 12207
(518) 463-3200
http://www.nysba.org

NORTH CAROLINA
North Carolina State Bar
208 Fayetteville Street Mall
Raleigh, NC 27601
mailing address:
PO Box 25908
Raleigh, NC 27611
(919) 828-4620

North Carolina Bar Association
1312 Annapolis Drive
Raleigh, NC 27608
mailing address:
PO Box 3688
Cary, NC 27519-3688
(919) 677-0561
http://www.ncbar.org

NORTH DAKOTA
State Bar Association of North Dakota
515 1/2 East Broadway, suite 101
Bismarck, ND 58501
mailing address:
PO Box 2136
Bismarck, ND 58502
(701) 255-1404

OHIO
Ohio State Bar Association
1700 Lake Shore Drive
Columbus, OH 43204
mailing address:
PO Box 16562
Columbus, OH 43216-6562
(614) 487-2050
http://www.ohiobar.org

OKLAHOMA
Oklahoma Bar Association
1901 North Lincoln
Oklahoma City, OK 73105
(405) 524-2365
http://www.okbar.org

OREGON

Oregon State Bar
5200 S.W. Meadows Road
PO Box 1689
Lake Oswego, OR 97035-0889
(503) 620-0222
http://www.osbar.org

PENNSYLVANIA

Pennsylvania Bar Association
100 South Street
PO Box 186
Harrisburg, PA 17108
(717) 238-6715
http://www.pabar.org

Pennsylvania Bar Institute
http://www.pbi.org

PUERTO RICO

Puerto Rico Bar Association
PO Box 1900
San Juan, Puerto Rico 00903
(787) 721-3358

RHODE ISLAND

Rhode Island Bar Association
115 Cedar Street
Providence, RI 02903
(401) 421-5740
http://www.ribar.org

SOUTH CAROLINA

South Carolina Bar
950 Taylor Street
PO Box 608
Columbia, SC 29202
(803) 799-6653
http://www.scbar.org

SOUTH DAKOTA

State Bar of South Dakota
222 East Capitol
Pierre, SD 57501
(605) 224-7554
http://www.sdbar.org

TENNESSEE

Tennessee Bar Assn
3622 West End Avenue
Nashville, TN 37205
(615) 383-7421
http://www.tba.org

TEXAS

State Bar of Texas
1414 Colorado
PO Box 12487
Austin, TX 78711
(512) 463-1463
http://www.texasbar.com/start.htm

UTAH

Utah State Bar
645 South 200 East, Suite 310
Salt Lake City, UT 84111
(801) 531-9077
http://www.utahbar.org

VERMONT

Vermont Bar Association
PO Box 100
Montpelier, VT 05601
(802) 223-2020
http://www.vtbar.org

Save On Legal Fees

with software and books from Made E-Z Products® available at your nearest bookstore, or call 1-800-822-4566

Everyday Law Made E-Z

The book that saves legal fees every time it's opened.

Here, in *Everyday Law Made E-Z*, are fast answers to 90% of the legal questions anyone is ever likely to ask, such as:

- How can I control my neighbor's pet?
- Can I change my name?
- What is a common law marriage?
- When should I incorporate my business?
- Is a child responsible for his bills?
- Who owns a husband's gifts to his wife?
- How do I become a naturalized citizen?
- Should I get my divorce in Nevada?
- Can I write my own will?
- Who is responsible when my son drives my car?
- How can my uncle get a Green Card?
- What are the rights of a non-smoker?
- Do I have to let the police search my car?
- What is sexual harassment?
- When is euthanasia legal?
- What repairs must my landlord make?
- What's the difference between fair criticism and slander?
- When can I get my deposit back?
- Can I sue the federal government?
- Am I responsible for a drunken guest's auto accident?
- Is a hotel liable if it does not honor a reservation?
- Does my car fit the lemon law?

Whether for personal or business use, this 500-page information-packed book helps the layman safeguard his property, avoid disputes, comply with legal obligations, and enforce his rights. Hundreds of cases illustrate thousands of points of law, each clearly and completely explained.

Stock No.: BK411
$24.95 8.5" x 11"
500 pages Soft cover

... Also available as software—Stock No. SW1185

MADE E-Z® PRODUCTS

MADE E·Z® KITS

$19.95

Each kit includes a clear, concise instructional manual to help you understand your rights and obligations, plus all the information and sample forms you need.

From the leaders in self-help legal products, it's quick, affordable, and it's E-Z.

Do-It-Yourself Kit
Last Will & Testament
Stock No. K307

$24.95 EACH
(except Last Will and Testament—$19.95)

MADE E-Z® PRODUCTS

...when you need it in writing!

Do-It-Yourself Kit
Incorporation
Stock No. K301

Do-It-Yourself Kit
Living Will
& Power of Attorney for Healthcare
Stock No. K306

Do-It-Yourself Kit
Buying/Selling Your Home
Stock No. K311

Do-It-Yourself Kit
Living Trust
Stock No. K305

Do-It-Yourself Kit
Credit Repair
Stock No. K303

Do-It-Yourself Kit
Limited Liability Company
Stock No. K316

Do-It-Yourself Kit
Business Startups
Stock No. K320

Do-It-Yourself Kit
Small Business/ Home Business
Stock No. K321

Do-It-Yourself Kit
Divorce
Stock No. K302

Do-It-Yourself Kit
Bankruptcy
Stock No. K300

ed 2002

Life Insurance Made E-Z

Life Insurance is the most common investment consumers make, However, most people buy life insurance without understanding how it works. Insurance companies are eliminating and selling coverage directly to consumers. Consumers now need to make life insurance decisions for themselves. *Life Insurance Made E-Z* helps make these decisions.

Essential subjects in the book:

- Why you need life insurance
- The general rules of life insurance
- Different types of coverage
- Who's involved in a life insurance contract
- Insurable interest
- The life insurance application
- Benefits of life insurance
- Considering other sources of protection
- Planning money for the long term
- Future college costs
- Naming and maintaining beneficiaries
- Exclusions and limitations
- Special family needs
- Using life insurance for medical treatment

. . . and much more.

Stock No.: G349
$14.95 6" x 9"
232 pages Soft cover

Made E-Z Products, Inc.
384 S. Military Trail
Deerfield Beach, FL 33442
(800) 822-4566 ❖ www.MadeE-Z.com

Synchronize home & office

from Made E-Z Products® call 1-800-822-4566

Your Profitable Home Business Made E-Z

The "must-have" book for anyone who works from home.

Here, in *Your Profitable Home Business Made E-Z*, are hundreds of the "hottest" and time-tested strategies for today's home-based worker, such as:

- Design and organize your workspace for maximum profit
- Turn your family into your biggest asset
- The 25 most important home office success tools
- Effectively sell yourself while you market your business
- Avoid common beginner's mistakes
- File and data management tips for greater profits
- Simple telecommunication tools to empower your office and productivity
- Successful strategies to stay motivated
- Health, computers, Zen and the home office
- Valuable must-have checklists and worksheets
- The fastest, easiest way to get into business . . . and out of the rat-race

Stock No.: SS4315
$24.95

Jeff Zbar, the "ChiefHomeOfficer.com," has worked as a home-based journalist, author, and small business advocate since the 1980s. In early 2001, he was named the U.S. Small Business Administration's 2001 Small Business Journalist of the Year.

MADE E-Z
PRODUCTS

	ITEM #	QTY.	PRICE‡	EXTENSION
MADE E-Z SOFTWARE				
E-Z Construction Estimator	SS4300		$29.95	
E-Z Contractors' Forms	SS4301		$24.95	
Contractors' Business Builder Bundle	CD325		$59.95	
Asset Protection	SS4304		$24.95	
Corporate Records	SS4305		$24.95	
Vital Records	SS4306		$24.95	
Personnel Forms	HR453		$24.95	
Accounting	SS4308		$24.95	
Limited Liability Companies (LLC)	SS4309		$24.95	
Partnerships	SS4310		$24.95	
Solving IRS Problems	SS4311		$24.95	
Winning In Small Claims Court	SS4312		$24.95	
Collecting Unpaid Bills	SS4313		$24.95	
Selling On The Web (E-Commerce)	SS4314		$24.95	
Your Profitable Home Business	SS4315		$24.95	
E-Z Business Lawyer Library	SS4318		$49.95	
E-Z Estate Planner	SS4319		$49.95	
E-Z Personal Lawyer Library	SS4320		$49.95	
Payroll	SS4321		$24.95	
Personal Legal Forms and Agreements	SS4322		$24.95	
Business Legal Forms and Agreements	SS4323		$24.95	
Employee Policies and Manuals	SS4324		$24.95	
Incorporation	SS4333		$24.95	
Last Wills	SS4327		$24.95	
Business Startups	SS4332		$24.95	
Credit Repair	SW2211		$24.95	
Business Forms	SW2223		$24.95	
Buying and Selling A Business	SW2242		$24.95	
Marketing Your Small Business	SW2245		$24.95	
Get Out Of Debt	SW2246		$24.95	
Winning Business Plans	SW2247		$24.95	
Successful Resumes	SW2248		$24.95	
Solving Business Problems	SW 2249		$24.95	
Profitable Mail Order	SW2250		$24.95	
Deluxe Business Forms	SW2251		$49.95	
E-Z Small Business Library	SW2252		$49.95	
Paint & Construction Estimator	SW2253		$19.95	
MADE E-Z BOOKS				
Bankruptcy	G300		$24.95	
Incorporation	G301		$24.95	
Divorce	G302		$24.95	
Credit Repair	G303		$14.95	
Living Trusts	G305		$24.95	
Living Wills	G306		$24.95	
Last Will & Testament	G307		$24.95	
Buying/Selling Your Home	G311		$14.95	
Employment Law	G312		$14.95	
Collecting Child Support	G315		$14.95	
Limited Liability Companies	G316		$24.95	
Partnerships	G318		$24.95	
Solving IRS Problems	G319		$14.95	
Asset Protection	G320		$14.95	
Buying/Selling A Business	G321		$14.95	
Financing Your Business	G322		$14.95	
Profitable Mail Order	G323		$14.95	
Selling On The Web (E-Commerce)	G324		$14.95	
SBA Loans	G325		$14.95	
Solving Business Problems	G326		$14.95	
Advertising Your Business	G327		$14.95	
Rapid Reading	G328		$14.95	
Everyday Math	G329		$14.95	
Shoestring Investing	G330		$14.95	
Stock Market Investing	G331		$14.95	
Fund Raising	G332		$14.95	
Money For College	G334		$14.95	
Marketing Your Small Business	G335		$14.95	

‡ *Prices are for a single item, and are subject to change without notice.*

MADE E-Z®
PRODUCTS

TO PLACE AN ORDER:

1. Duplicate this order form.

2. Complete your order and mail or fax to:

Made E-Z® Products, Inc.

384 S. Military Trail
Deerfield Beach, FL 33442

www.MadeE-Z.com

Telephone:
954-480-8933

Toll Free:
800-822-4566

Fax:
954-480-8906

continued on next page

ed 2002

Whatever you need to know, we've made it E-Z!

Informative text and forms you can fill out on-screen.* From personal to business, legal to leisure—we've made it E-Z!

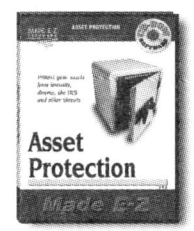

- Get Out Of Debt
- Credit Repair
- Vital Records

Personal & Family

For all your family's needs, we have titles that will help keep you organized and guide you through most every aspect of your personal life.

- Living Wills
- Asset Protection
- Buying/Selling Your Home

Business

Whether you're starting from scratch with a home business or you just want to keep your corporate records in shape, we've got the programs for you.

- Incorporation
- Corporate Records
- Accounting
- Your Profitable Home Business
- Selling on the Web (E-Commerce)
- Advertising Your Business

* Not all titles include forms   ed 2002

E-Z to load, E-Z to run, E-Z to use!

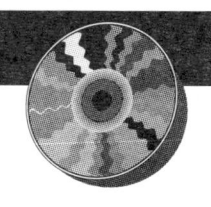

For our complete list of titles, call 1-800-822-4566
or visit our web site: www.MadeE-Z.com

Legal

Easy to understand text explains how to fill out and file forms to perform all the legal tasks you need to— without all those costly legal fees!

- Everyday Legal Forms & Agreements
- Bankruptcy
- Everyday Law
- Living Trusts
- Divorce
- Last Wills

Financial

Make smart investment decisions to secure your financial future. Expert advice to make more money, and keep and protect more of what you have made.

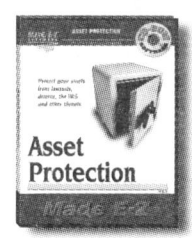

- Stock Market Investing
- Mutual Fund Investing
- Shoestring Investing
- Offshore Investing
- Asset Protection
- Financing Your Business

MADE E-Z
PRODUCTS®

Made E-Z Products, 384 S. Military Trail, Deerfield Beach, FL 33442
(800) 822-4566 • fax: (954) 480-8906
web site: http://www.MadeE-Z.com

ed 2002

	ITEM #	QTY.	PRICE‡	EXTENSION
Owning A No-Cash-Down Business	G336		$14.95	
Offshore Investing	G337		$14.95	
Multi-level Marketing	G338		$14.95	
Free Legal Help	G339		$14.95	
Get Out Of Debt	G340		$14.95	
Winning Business Plans	G342		$14.95	
Mutual Fund Investing	G343		$14.95	
Business Startups	G344		$14.95	
Successful Resumes	G346		$14.95	
Free Stuff For Everyone	G347		$14.95	
On-Line Business Resources	G348		$14.95	
Life Insurance	G349		$14.95	
Health Insurance	G350		$14.95	
Successful Selling	G351		$14.95	
Everyday Legal Forms & Agreements	BK407		$24.95	
Personnel Forms	BK408		$24.95	
Collecting Unpaid Bills	BK409		$24.95	
Corporate Records	BK410		$24.95	
Everyday Law	BK411		$24.95	
Vital Records	BK412		$24.95	
Business Forms	BK414		$24.95	

MADE E-Z KITS

Bankruptcy Kit	K300		$24.95	
Incorporation Kit	K301		$24.95	
Divorce Kit	K302		$24.95	
Credit Repair Kit	K303		$24.95	
Living Trust Kit	K305		$24.95	
Living Will Kit	K306		$24.95	
Last Will & Testament Kit	K307		$19.95	
Buying and Selling Your Home Kit	K311		$24.95	
Business Startups Kit	K320		$24.95	
Small Business/Home Business Kit	K321		$24.95	

MISC. PRODUCTS

☆ Federal Labor Law Poster	LP001		$5.99	
☆ State Specific Labor Law Poster (see state listings below)			$29.95	
E-Z Legal Will Pac	WP250		$9.95	

State	Item#	QTY	State	Item#	QTY	State	Item#	QTY
AL	83801		KY	83817		ND	83834	
AK	83802		LA	83818		OH	83835	
AZ	83803		ME	83819		OK	83836	
AR	83804		MD	83820		OR	83837	
CA	83805		MA	83821		PA	83838	
CO	83806		MI	83822		RI	83839	
CT	83807		MN	83823		SC	83840	
DE	83808		MS	83824		S. Dakota not available		
DC	83848		MO	83825		TN	83842	
FL	83809		MT	83826		TX	83843	
GA	83810		NE	83827		UT	83844	
HI	83811		NV	83828		VT	83845	
ID	83812		NH	83829		VA	83846	
IL	83813		NJ	83830		WA	83847	
IN	83814		NM	83831		WV	83849	
IO	83815		NY	83832		WI	83850	
KS	83816		NC	83833		WY	83851	

ORDER TOTAL ☆ Required by Federal & State Laws	$
SHIPPING & HANDLING $4.95 for first item, $1.50 for each additional item (All orders shipped Ground unless otherwise specified)	$
SUBTOTAL	$
Florida Residents add 6% sales tax	$
TOTAL	$

SS 2001 r4

‡ Prices are for a single item, and are subject to change without notice.

MADE E-Z PRODUCTS

PLEASE COMPLETE THE FOLLOWING INFORMATION:

NAME: _____

COMPANY: _____

ADDRESS: _____

CITY: _____

STATE: _____ ZIP: _____

PHONE: ( ) _____

PAYMENT METHOD:

☐ Charge my credit card:
  ☐ MasterCard
  ☐ VISA
  ☐ American Express

ACCOUNT NO.
[ ][ ][ ][ ][ ][ ][ ][ ][ ][ ][ ][ ][ ][ ][ ][ ]

EXP DATE [ ][ ][ ][ ]

SIGNATURE _____ (required for credit card purchases)

☐ Check enclosed, payable to:

**Made E-Z Products, Inc.
384 S. Military Trail
Deerfield Beach, FL 33442**

Company Purchase Orders Are Welcome With Approved Credit

Index

A-D

acceptance 84
accountant 19
acknowledgement 58
action 77
advertising and promotion 47-51
Arm & Hammer 145
artists 33
bankruptcy 50
benefits 27
business plan 31-33, 185-189
casinos 30
celebration 63
change 82-84
concept 42
confrontation 117
control 108
credit 47
customer financing 194
debt 194
defining moments 86-87
Degeorge, Gail 15
delegating 34
desire 61
details 39
diligence 62
Disney World 37
Disney, Walt 139
divorce 177
dot.coms 38
Drucker, Peter 26
Durocher, Leo 14

229

E-M

Eastman, George 144
education 57
Entrepreneurial Fever 13
Entrepreneurial Spirit... 56
errors 24
ethics 178
fame 140
fatalist 108-109
fear 111
Federal Express 17
financial risk tolerance 174
forgiveness 80
future 150
Heinz, R. J. 25
hiring 34
honesty 77
implementers 15
Industrial Revolution 146
innovators 14
integrity 77
intrapreneur 164
intuition 68
inventors 15
investors 189
Johnson & Johnson 37
juicers 27
landscaping 28
leadership 35
managing 33
Mercedes-Benz 49
Michener, James 34
Mozart, Wolfgang Amadeus 152
musicians 33

Index

O-W

on-the-job training ... 29
Patterson, Clare ... 131
perks ... 44
Personal Mapping ... 69-73
prioritizing ... 155-162
profit level ... 30
release ... 78
risk ... 15-20
    high ... 17
    low ... 19
    medium ... 18
rolodex ... 147
Roosevelt, Franklin D. ... 79
sales and collections ... 46-47
salesman ... 35
SBA loans ... 190
Schumpeter, Joseph ... 14
scrapbooks ... 26
self-confidence ... 106, 133
self-doubt ... 44
self-evaluation ... 61
spirit ... 55
Thomas, Dave ... 120, 130
Titanic ... 38
Transmedia Network ... 18
Truman, Harry ... 79
truth ... 73-75
value-added inducements ... 49
venture capitalists ... 192
will ... 59
Wright, Frank Lloyd ... 121, 129
Wrigley, William ... 149